D0771189

DISCARD

WEAPONS: DESIGNING THE TOOLS OF WAR

The USS Maine, *an Ohio-class strategic-missile submarine launched in 1994, carries 192 nuclear warheads that have a nearly 5,000-mile range.*

WEAPONS:
DESIGNING
THE
TOOLS OF WAR

Jason Richie

SAN LEANDRO
LIBRARY
HIGH SCHOOL

The Oliver Press, Inc.
Minneapolis

Copyright © 2000 by The Oliver Press, Inc.

All rights reserved.
No part of this book may be reproduced in any form or by
any means without permission in writing from the publisher.
Please address inquiries to:

The Oliver Press, Inc.
Charlotte Square
5707 West 36th Street
Minneapolis, MN 55416-2510

*The author wishes to thank naval historian Edwyn Gray for his
careful reading of the chapter on Robert Whitehead. Gray's book,*
**The Devil's Device: Robert Whitehead and the History of the
Torpedo,** *was indispensable to the chapter, and any remaining
shortcomings are the author's alone.*

Library of Congress Cataloging-in-Publication Data
Richie, Jason, 1966-
Weapons : designing the tools of war / Jason Richie.
p.   cm. — (Innovators ; 7)
Includes bibliographical references and index.
        Summary: Traces the development of weapons through the
lives of such inventors and their inventions as David Bushnell and the
submarine, Samuel Colt and the revolver, John Ericsson and the
battleship, Hiram Maxim and the machine gun, and Ernest Swinton
and the tank.
ISBN 1-881508-60-9 (lib. bdg.)
1. Military weapons—History—Juvenile literature. 2. Warships—
History—Juvenile literature. 3. Inventors—Biography—Juvenile
literature. [1. Military weapons. 2. Inventors.] I. Title. II.
Series.
U815.R53 2000
623—dc21   98-53190
                                                                  CIP
                                                                  AC
ISBN 1-881508-60-9
Printed in the United States of America

06 05 04 03 02 01 00   8 7 6 5 4 3 2 1

CONTENTS

INTRODUCTION   Finding the Target   7

CHAPTER ONE   David Bushnell
                      and the Submarine   17

CHAPTER TWO   Samuel Colt
                      and the Revolver   31

CHAPTER THREE   John Ericsson
                      and the Battleship   45

CHAPTER FOUR   Robert Whitehead
                      and the Torpedo   59

CHAPTER FIVE   Hiram Maxim
                      and the Automatic Machine Gun   75

CHAPTER SIX   Ernest Swinton
                      and the Tank   89

CHAPTER SEVEN   Walter Dornberger and Wernher von Braun
                      and the Ballistic Missile   105

AFTERWORD   Weapons of the Future   123

                      Glossary   129

                      Bibliography   135

                      Index   139

Finding the Target

What is the most destructive power in history? Is it the tank with the thermal-imaging sight that senses an enemy vehicle's heat so it can see—and kill—even in total darkness? Is it a rocket torpedo that shoots straight to the surface from a submarine, flies through the air toward an enemy sub, and then dives at its target? Maybe it's the electrically powered machine gun that churns out 110 rounds per second—yes, per second—to obliterate its opponent with a blast straight out of a science-fiction movie. Then again, it's probably an intercontinental ballistic missile (ICBM) armed with nuclear warheads.

Actually, it's none of these. We have to go all the way back to the beginning of weapons development, when people first figured out that certain devices made warfare a lot more effective. A person's arm, for example, could not cast a stone very far, so someone somewhere devised a leather sling that multiplied that distance and speed. Elsewhere, another person extended the range of a sharpened stick used for thrusting by picking it up and throwing

Although weapons have surpassed them in lethality, the atomic bombs dropped on Hiroshima and Nagasaki in Japan are the deadliest weapons ever used in action. Close to 100,000 people were killed by the two bombs in August 1945.

it. When people learned to work with bronze around 3000 B.C., they increased their spears' killing efficiency by adding metal tips.

None of these primitive tools could be considered the most destructive, so we'll keep looking. When the legions of Julius Caesar took to the field in the first century B.C., they used improved spears, which they called javelins. The creative Romans attached thin cords to their javelins. When yanked at the moment of release, the cords imparted a spin to the javelin that improved its range and accuracy.

Since 1200 B.C., people had known how to form iron into swords. By Caesar's day, the sword had been refined into the two-foot-long gladius, the perfect thrusting weapon for hand-to-hand combat. Then there were the ingenious catapults. First developed in 399 B.C., these mechanical artillery pieces derived their "shooting" power from springs, twisted bundles of cords, or heavy counterweights. The largest devices launched 600-pound stones over the walls of forts. Smaller models flung bundles of flaming arrows at foes. Caesar even used catapults to toss corpses into enemy camps to spread disease.

Cavalry troops with swords, lances, and bows also marched for Caesar and his contemporaries. First used around 1000 B.C., these soldiers on horseback rode near the infantry, gathering information and providing security for the soldiers on foot. They also spearheaded major assaults, often in horse-drawn battle vehicles known as chariots. No matter what the situation demanded, clever innovators always supplied just the right weapons.

Leading his troops into Britain in 55 B.C., Julius Caesar wielded two gladius swords. In the background, javelins rain through the air at the enemy.

When the twisted ropes on catapults such as this one were released, they could launch a stone weighing up to 50 pounds as far as the length of four football fields.

Still don't know the answer to our question? Let's keep looking. As weapons improved through the ages, so did people's ability to defend themselves. Body armor was adopted as blacksmiths developed greater skill at working with metals. Protective coverings of leather or wood gave way to iron chain mail by A.D. 1000, which in turn was replaced with complete suits of armor by the 1350s. With the improvement in armor, battle casualties dropped. But what if a heavily armored knight fell from his horse? Barely able to crawl with all the extra weight, the man was an easy target.

To overcome these improved defenses, armies demanded better weapons. By the mid-1200s, English craftsmen had lengthened the common bow a foot or so to about six feet. With the increased power of their "longbows," skilled archers could hit enemy columns 280 yards away. Crossbows of wood,

Fired from the shoulder, the **crossbow** was a small bow set crossways on a wooden handle, or **stock**.

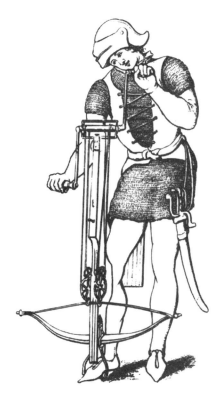

The archer cranked back the crossbow mechanically to achieve greater tension and thus power than possible when pulling back by hand. The bow could then be fired with the release of the trigger.

If you undertake a task "lock, stock, and barrel," that means you go at it with your whole effort. Together, the lock, stock, and barrel make up the essential parts of a gun.

first used by Chinese warriors in 500 B.C., were being fitted with steel bows by the early 1300s. Extreme ranges of 380 yards were now possible with the shoulder-fired missile launchers. Both longbows and crossbows could penetrate armor.

Attacking forces grew even stronger when Europeans learned to harness the power of an explosive mixture invented by the Chinese. First made known to Europe in 1242 by the English monk Roger Bacon, the explosive acquired the name gunpowder from the first guns in the 1320s. When ignited in the open end of an otherwise closed tube, gunpowder hurled stones with lethal force. No longer did troops have to rely on mechanical devices like catapults or their own muscle power to kill. Humans' destructive ability skyrocketed.

The first handguns were nothing more than one- to three-foot-long barrels of iron or brass attached to wooden poles. The gunner grasped the pole with one hand, using the other hand to ignite the gunpowder through a touchhole. The touchhole was located at the closed end of the barrel (the breech). Because of the clumsy and difficult process, early firearms were much less lethal than the crossbow, longbow, spear, or sword.

But performance improved as handguns evolved. Innovators replaced the poles with wooden handles called stocks, which permitted the gun to be fired from the shoulder like the crossbow. In 1411, the matchlock appeared. It was a short lever attached to the breech that held a piece of slow-burning twine. When pushed forward, the lit twine—or match—ignited a bit of gunpowder sprin-kled in a small pan beside the touchhole. The flash of the "priming" powder then traveled through the touchhole to set off the gun's main powder charge that was packed within the breech.

Guns improved as soldiers discovered better ways to ignite the main charge. The wheellock, introduced in the late 1400s, relied on sparks created when a piece of iron pyrite rubbed against a small, rough-edged wheel—a mechanism similar to that found in modern-day cigarette lighters. The pyrite was held in the jaws of a "cock," a finger-sized metal lever located behind the touchhole. Before each shot, the gunner used his thumb to pull back the cock. Although the wheellock worked, soldiers needed a less delicate device for the battlefield.

The flintlock, invented a century later by the Dutch, was more durable. Instead of iron pyrite, the jaws of the cock grasped a miniscule wedge of flint. When the gunner pulled the trigger, the cock

Something is called a "flash in the pan" if its success or popularity was short-lived. The phrase is as old as the matchlock, which first employed a priming pan beside the touchhole. Often the flash of the priming powder failed to ignite the main charge, making it a "flash in the pan."

One problem with the matchlock system was that the gunner needed a lit match to be ready to fire—this was difficult in wet weather and revealed the soldier's location at night.

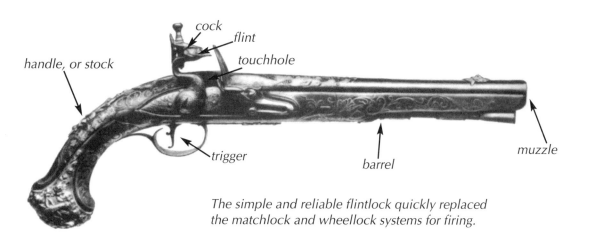

The simple and reliable flintlock quickly replaced the matchlock and wheellock systems for firing.

Flint is a kind of quartz that produces sparks when struck against steel.

The matchlock, wheellock, flintlock, and early percussion guns are all **muzzle-loading** firearms, which means that the gunpowder and round are loaded with a tool called a ramrod through the open end of the barrel. Guns that are loaded through the closed end of the barrel are called **breech-loading** firearms.

One major advance in guns was the **rifled bore**, first invented in the fifteenth century and used in most firearms (not just rifles) since the mid-1800s. When the inside of a gun's barrel, or bore, is rifled, grooves are carved in it. The gunfire is more powerful than in the smooth-bore shotgun because the fired bullet expands into the grooves and fits tighter, and it is also more accurate because of the stabilizing spin imparted to the bullet when shot.

snapped forward like a rooster (hence its name) to peck a steel plate directly above the priming pan. Sparks rained down and ignited the primer. Easy to operate and tough enough for battlefield use, flint-lock weapons became the standard firearm for the next two centuries. Only when a minister named Alexander Forsyth patented the "percussion" system in 1807 was the way cleared for others to invent multi-shot revolvers and rapid-fire machine guns.

Samuel Colt was the first innovator to hit the financial bull's-eye using Forsyth's invention. In 1836, he received a patent on the first practical repeating firearm. But even this weapon ultimately proved to be too slow. As nations demanded something faster, Hiram Maxim responded in 1884 with a rapid-fire gun so horribly effective that it literally forced soldiers underground into trenches. When Ernest Swinton unveiled the tank in 1916 during World War I, the huddled infantry once again had the capacity to charge their enemies.

After its defeat in World War I, Germany was stripped of its long-range bombers and artillery pieces. This led innovators Walter Dornberger and Wernher von Braun to develop a new type of rocket-propelled artillery now known as the ballistic missile. Today's ballistic missile, when topped with one or more nuclear warheads, is certainly a good candidate for our most destructive power.

But wait, the story isn't over. At sea, admirals have also demanded improved tools of war. While oar-powered ships dominated naval battles from the eighth century B.C. until about 400 years ago, they eventually fell from favor because of a pair of innovations. The first was improved sails and rigging, which allowed ships to maneuver effectively and to sail into the wind if necessary.

The other advance was the introduction of the port—a hole in the side of a ship through which cargo was loaded. Ingenious boat designers quickly adapted artillery to fire through the portholes. Previously, cannons mounted on the uppermost deck could actually capsize a vessel if too many along one side were fired at once. This was because the force of the cannon fire made the deck—and thus the whole ship—rock backward. In contrast, cannons discharged through the portholes presented little

This warship shows cannons mounted below deck, on what came to be known as the gun deck. They were shot through portholes spread along the side of the ship.

threat of overturning the ship because of their lower center of gravity. With improved sails and port-firing cannons, "broadside" sailing ships ruled the seas after the late 1500s. By the 1850s, the typical triple-decker, wooden-hulled broadside carried over 100 guns and needed no other power than the wind.

Still, improvements kept coming. Robert Fulton had invented the first steam-powered warship in 1814, providing an alternative to sails. When Henri-Joseph Paixhans devised the explosive cannon-shell in 1837, ships needed greater protection for their vulnerable wooden sides. John Ericsson responded by introducing the ironclad *Monitor* in 1862. Even with just two cannons, Ericsson's unique boat was the most dangerous afloat because its guns were housed inside a revolving turret, an innovation that allowed the *Monitor* to shoot from any angle.

The battleships that followed, even the monster Japanese models of World War II, were never as dominant as the broadsides because of another new weapon. In the late 1860s, Robert Whitehead introduced a self-propelled torpedo capable of blowing any ship out of the water. Ship builders struck back, designing torpedo-boat "destroyers." The destroyers then came under fire from submarines that fired their torpedoes beneath the waves.

Submarine warfare was nothing new. In 1776, during the Revolutionary War, American David Bushnell had been the first to use an underwater warship. Combined with Whitehead's torpedo by World War I, subs were more lethal than ever. And they have only become deadlier. Today's submarines

can fire rocket-powered torpedoes at other seacraft, and they can target cities thousands of miles away with nuclear-armed ballistic missiles.

So, knowing all this, what is the world's most destructive power? Is it the tank, the machine gun, or the submarine? Or is it a warship, a torpedo, or a swarm of ballistic missiles? No, it's none of these. History's most destructive power is the human capacity to innovate. Throughout history, people have used their ingenuity to design remarkable devices that sustain and improve life—artificial hearts, microscopes, and lightning-quick computer chips. Side by side with these magnificent inventions, however, brilliant innovators have designed the most terrible tools of war.

A Subroc (submarine rocket) missile, a modern-day torpedo, is fired from a submarine. Subroc is a solid-fuel rocket with a nuclear warhead designed to destroy an enemy submarine.

CHAPTER ONE

David Bushnell and the Submarine

After a second explosion ripped through the hull of the Union ship *Housatonic* on February 17, 1864, Lieutenant G. E. Dixon of the Confederate navy knew he and his crew had just made history. Dixon's submarine, the *H. L. Hunley*, had just delivered a spar torpedo—an explosive keg on the end of a long pole, or "spar." Since the torpedo struck just below the *Housatonic's* ammunition hold, the second eruption was even more spectacular than the first. As the stricken ship went down in the harbor of Charleston, South Carolina, the *Hunley* became the first submarine to sink an enemy ship.

Dixon's exhausted crew never got the chance to celebrate. Following their success, they backed off a safe distance and surfaced, then opened their hatches on top for some fresh air. A Union rescue ship, the *Canandaigua*, picked that moment to steam past on its way to the doomed *Housatonic*. Before Dixon could sound the alarm, water from the steamer's

No portrait was ever painted of David Bushnell (1740-1826), but a nineteenth-century historian drew his submarine. This drawing shows screw propellers (top and right) in error. Bushnell's actual submarine did not use this type of propeller.

It was no surprise that the Hunley went down. One of a small fleet of Confederate submarines, the Hunley had sunk three previous times in trials, drowning its crew each time. The sub's inventor, H. L. Hunley, was one of the victims.

---

mine: an explosive inside a container. In Bushnell's time, wooden kegs were the usual containers.

---

wake flooded the *Hunley*'s hatches. The sub went down and all aboard drowned. Thus, the *Hunley* also become the first submarine lost in battle.

While the *Hunley*'s demise can be blamed on several technological shortcomings (and a devastating dose of bad luck), its successful attack can be traced to one individual—David Bushnell. Almost 90 years earlier, during the Revolutionary War, the 36-year-old colonist's revolutionary sub, the *Turtle*, attempted the first underwater attack. Bushnell pioneered undersea warfare by inventing a submarine that used a new form of propulsion. To make his sub lethal, he also developed underwater mines.

David Bushnell was born on August 30, 1740, on a farm near Saybrook, Connecticut. The first of five children, David was six years old when his brother, Ezra, was born. Three sisters followed.

Growing up, David helped his father around the farm and usually spent any spare time reading. Unfortunately, with a struggling farm, there wasn't much time to spare. College seemed out of the question. As the oldest son, David resigned himself to working the farm to help support his family.

In 1767, tragedy struck the Bushnells when David's father and two of his sisters died. But out of the misfortune came opportunity. David's mother soon remarried and took her youngest daughter to her new home, leaving the farm to her two sons. With no one left to care for but himself, David sold his share of the farm to Ezra. Finally, in 1771, the 31-year-old Bushnell entered Yale College (now Yale University) in New Haven, Connecticut.

It was at Yale that Bushnell first considered building an undersea warship. The idea was not new. In 1578, William Bourne of England insisted it was possible to build a completely new type of boat that could dive beneath the water "unto the bottom" and surface again at will. For the next 200 years, innovators strived to turn Bourne's theory into reality. Most dreamed of using the sub in war.

Bourne's apparent plan was to use flexible leather walls that could be collapsed to allow water in so the craft would sink and expanded to push the water out so the vessel would rise again.

Cornelius Drebbel of Holland, for instance, used Bourne's writings as a guide when he built the first workable submarine in 1623. With the sub as his delivery vehicle, Drebbel hoped to ram explosives into unsuspecting enemy ships. His vessel was essentially two rowboats attached together, one upside down atop the other. Drebbel wrapped the whole contraption in a tight leather skin to lock out water. For propulsion, 12 oars protruded from the sides, their holes made watertight with sleeves of greased leather. While the submarine made at least one short voyage at a depth of 15 feet, there is no evidence that Drebbel developed any explosive device for it.

In the 1690s, mathematician Denis Papin of Germany designed two submarines—first a metal version, then a wood—that used oars to move under water. For depth control, Papin chose Bourne's method of using water as ballast. If he wanted the sub to dive, he pumped water in; pumping it back out allowed the craft to surface. Papin even devised a gauge to measure depth. The boat's weaponry was not so well thought out, however. Papin said only that crew members would reach through watertight armholes to "touch enemy vessels and ruin them." Unfortunately, his first boat was destroyed during a test and the second was never finished.

Papin may have modeled his teapot-shaped subs after a pressure cooker he had invented. Later, in 1707, Papin was the first person to successfully launch a steamboat.

In 1653, a French inventor named de Son designed this wooden submarine armed with iron bars on each end for ramming other ships. The paddle wheel, powered by a weak clockwork engine, could not budge the vessel.

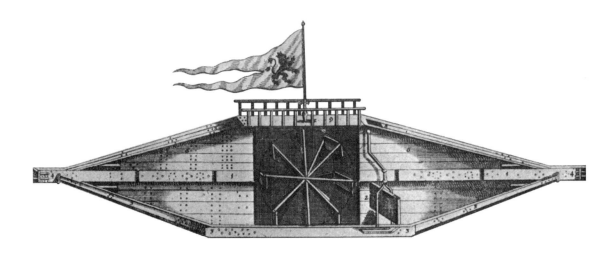

The next to try his hand at building an underwater warship was Johann Christian Pretorius of Germany. In 1772, he launched a giant, fish-shaped boat, complete with a tail that was supposed to move side to side and propel the craft beneath the surface. Pretorius armed his submarine with a traditional cannon. Since guns were useless underwater, the inventor probably planned to fire the cannon once his craft had surfaced alongside an enemy. While the wooden fish did float when tested, there is no evidence that it moved or that any underwater test or attack occurred.

Just one year after Pretorius's experiments, wagon-maker J. Day dived with his wooden sub to a depth of 30 feet in a river near the coast of England. Then, in 1774, Day took his boat to a spot where he knew the depth was greater than 130 feet. His submarine, weighted down with stones as ballast, dropped from sight. But before Day could operate the mechanism that released the stones, the rapidly increasing water pressure crushed its wooden hull. Day's sub and his body were never recovered.

ballast: anything heavy carried in a submarine, ship, or hot-air balloon to provide stability and sometimes depth control. In a sub, ballast is usually water. It is allowed in to make the vessel sink and pumped out to make it rise.

Day's tragedy was a grim lesson to future submariners about the danger of water pressure. The work of previous experimenters offered other valuable revelations. Some concepts, like Bourne's idea of using water ballast to control depth, proved effective. Other ideas, like propelling vessels under water with paddle wheels or oars, were either impractical or downright useless.

In addition to the challenge of creating a workable underwater vehicle, some practical means of destroying enemy ships had to be discovered if the craft was to be an effective weapon. Ramming would be too dangerous for a sub, and explosives could only be used for attacks above the water, where a sub would be as vulnerable as, well, a fish out of water. As things stood in the mid-1770s, underwater warfare was still nothing more than a fantasy.

Enter David Bushnell, ready to make his mark on the world in the area of undersea warfare. While at Yale, he exploded small gunpowder-filled kegs under water. Bushnell also showed that a big enough bomb—which he called a "sub-marine mine"—could be quite destructive. Once Bushnell built the mine—a 150-pound keg of gunpowder that was detonated by a clock-activated flintlock mechanism—he designed a "sub-marine vessel" to attach the unique explosive to enemy ships.

The vessel Bushnell built soon after graduating from Yale in spring 1775 borrowed heavily from Papin's submarine. Water was again the ballast of choice. Like Papin, Bushnell pumped water in to make his boat sink and pumped it out when he was ready to surface. Bushnell's sub had a depth gauge and brass tubes to breathe through when the craft was close enough to the surface—just like Papin's vessel. It's probable Bushnell had heard of Day's tragic demise, because the new submarine utilized internal braces to prevent the sides from being crushed by the water's pressure. The one thing Bushnell could not borrow from Papin or anyone else was the mode of propulsion. Bushnell needed something new—but what?

Bushnell's term, from *sub*, Latin for under, and *marine*, meaning water, has stood the test of time.

THE BREAKTHROUGH

Bushnell's solution was as ingenious as it was simple. For centuries, people had known that wind would drive the arms of a windmill, but apparently no one before Bushnell had thought of using the windmill itself as the driving force. By attaching two oars together to operate like windmill blades, which would be cranked by hand instead of blown by the wind, Bushnell created his propellers. There was only one thing left to do—name his submarine. Since the craft looked like two turtle shells joined together, Bushnell called it the *Turtle*.

Bushnell's anticipated method of attack was straightforward. First, the *Turtle* would drift or be towed on the surface as close to the enemy as possible without being detected. Then, by pumping a valve with his foot and cranking a vertical propeller, the operator would dive. A forward propeller would move the sub underneath the target's hull. Once in place, the submariner would use the *Turtle*'s top-mounted drill to insert a hook into the ship's wooden planking. Attached to this hook was the mine, which the operator would arm by pulling a cord as he moved away. Thirty minutes later—BOOM! If it worked as Bushnell planned, the enemy vessel would sink and he would make history.

His chance came in 1776, after the American colonies declared independence from England. Bushnell offered his submarine to colonial leaders and won over the skeptics who doubted the effectiveness of underwater explosives with a spectacular

A replica of Bushnell's Turtle. *Squeezed into a chamber six feet tall and three feet wide, the operator had to breathe through a tube while maneuvering the hand and foot controls.*

George Washington had been commander in chief of the American forces for over a year in September 1776.

demonstration. It was enough to impress General George Washington, who gave Bushnell the go-ahead for an attack.

By then, almost 300 British warships occupied New York City's harbor. Bushnell's target was the fleet commander's 64-gun ship, the *Eagle*, which was moored off the island where the Statue of Liberty now stands. Before dawn on September 7, 1776, a couple rowboats towed the *Turtle* into position.

The man Bushnell had trained to operate the tiny submarine was army sergeant Ezra Lee. After Lee dropped inside the sub and secured the hatch, he cranked the forward windmill-type propeller until he was just short of the *Eagle*. As he pumped the foot-controlled valve and turned the vertical propeller, the *Turtle* slipped beneath the surface of the pitch-black water. From previous tests, Lee knew he had only 30 minutes of air.

Thanks to his glowing depth gauge, which Bushnell had fashioned from a luminescent wood fungus, Lee could tell when he was deep enough. Once under the *Eagle*, however, he hit iron—either a bolt or a strap supporting the ship's rudder—with his drill bit. Desperately, Lee shifted a few inches, only to lose contact with the *Eagle* altogether. His labored cranking of the drill and propellers had eaten away at his oxygen supply, and Lee began to feel woozy. He had no choice but to break off the attack and surface.

When he popped his hatch, Lee was chagrined to discover that daylight had broken. The British were on the lookout and spotted the bobbing submarine. A British boat stormed after the intruder. Cranking for all he was worth, Sergeant Lee released the mine in the path of his pursuers. His load lightened by 150 pounds, Lee was able to escape. The mine exploded an hour later, harming no one, but it was enough to convince the British to anchor their ships farther away from shore.

Sometime during the next month, Lee made at least one more attack in the *Turtle*. It, too, failed. On October 6, Bushnell's sub was lost when the boat transporting it was sunk by a British ship. While the *Turtle* was recovered a short time later, it never fought again. As Bushnell explained, "I waited for a more favorable opportunity, which never arrived."

Robert Fulton (1765-1815) was not only a great inventor, he was also a painter and a friend of the best artists and writers of his time.

THE RESULT

While it did not sink its target, the *Turtle* proved that submarine warfare was possible. Washington himself characterized Lee's attack as "an effort of genius" that failed because too many things had to go right against "an enemy who are always on guard."

Another person who noticed Bushnell's genius was fellow American Robert Fulton. Now known principally for his development of the first practical steamboat in 1807, Fulton was also one of history's greatest innovators of naval weapons. Besides introducing the first steam warship in 1814, he broke new ground in the realm of underwater weaponry. On June 13, 1800, he launched a submarine called the *Nautilus*, a name later immortalized by novelist Jules Verne in *Twenty Thousand Leagues under the Sea*.

While Fulton borrowed much from Bushnell's craft—ballast pumps, hand-cranked propellers, and underwater mines—his submarine was very different. For instance, to aid his sub's underwater maneuverability, Fulton shaped it like a cigar. For improved depth control, he ditched Bushnell's vertical propeller and attached a horizontal wing to the steering rudder. Now called a diving plane, Fulton's wing can still be found on modern submarines. Fulton also invented a tank filled with compressed air that extended the dive time for the sub's four-man crew—a device that might have changed history had Sergeant Lee had one in 1776. Finally, after discovering that compasses worked just as well under water, Fulton included one of those, too.

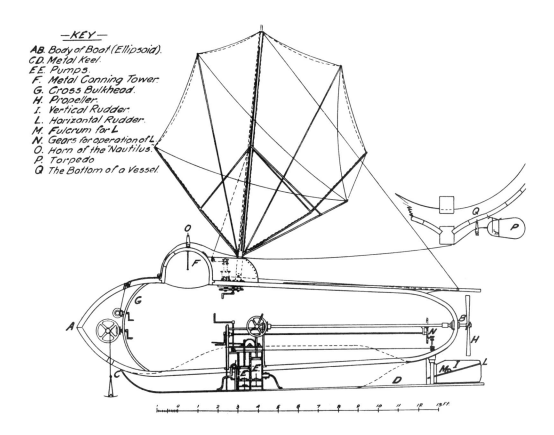

—KEY—
AB. Body of Boat (Ellipsoid).
CD. Metal Keel.
EE. Pumps.
 F. Metal Conning Tower.
 G. Cross Bulkhead.
 H. Propeller.
 I. Vertical Rudder.
 L. Horizontal Rudder.
 M. Fulcrum for L.
 N. Gears for operation of L.
 O. Horn of the "Nautilus."
 P. Torpedo
 Q. The Bottom of a Vessel.

But to be a weapon, the sub needed effective underwater explosives. Fulton again used Bushnell's designs as a guide. He tested *Turtle*-type clockwork mines and experimented with bombs that exploded on impact. Fulton also introduced a new type of "bomb submarine" that floated just below the surface, held in place by an anchor. He called these "torpedoes" after a type of stinging fish. In a test on October 15, 1804, Fulton used two time-fused torpedoes to sink a ship. It was the first time any vessel had been destroyed by an underwater explosion.

Fulton's 1798 design of the Nautilus *shows a collapsible mast and sail for surface travel and a windmill propeller (H) for moving under water. Notice the submarine's "torpedo" (P)— an underwater explosive— attaching to the hull of an enemy ship (Q).*

Despite the destructive potential of the submarine and torpedoes, Fulton found few takers. As early as December 1797, he had offered his planned submarine to France to defeat the English navy. He completed the *Nautilus* in 1800 and began testing it and then making improvements. By 1801, however, Napoleon Bonaparte was negotiating peace with England and did not want to "torpedo" the talks. Napoleon rejected Fulton's explosives and refused to pay him to build more submarines.

The Napoleonic Wars erupted in 1803, and Fulton sailed to England the next year to offer his devices to France's enemy. English interest dried up after their fleet annihilated the French navy at the Battle of Trafalgar in October 1805. Frustrated, Fulton returned to his home in the United States and turned his attention to surface steamships.

David Bushnell had long since retired by then. After attacking the British fleet with floating mines in 1777, Bushnell was captured. Upon his release, he continued fighting the British until the American Revolution ended in 1783. Four years later, for unknown reasons, Bushnell dropped out of sight. There is some evidence that he met Fulton in Europe sometime between 1787 and 1795, so the two may have discussed submarine warfare. After 1795, Bushnell returned to the United States and settled in Georgia under the name Bush. For a time, he worked as a schoolteacher and physician. He died in 1826.

David Bushnell's legacy lives on. Since their successful use in the Civil War, submarines have

While Fulton's *Nautilus* did not see action, the U.S. Navy picked up the name for its first nuclear-powered submarine, which was launched in 1954. This new *Nautilus's* fuel system allowed it to travel at full speed four times longer than traditional subs.

evolved into awesome weapons. For example, there are two nuclear-powered Seawolfs now in service in the United States Navy. The Seawolfs are primarily designed to hunt and kill surface ships and other subs, but they can also lay mines and transport commando teams.

As deadly as a Seawolf-class attack sub is, its firepower pales in comparison with one of America's 18 Ohio-class ballistic-missile submarines. Each sub can launch 24 Trident C-4 missiles capable of hitting any target within a 4,850 mile range—roughly twice the distance from New York to San Francisco. Since each Trident missile carries 8 nuclear warheads, that's 192 nuclear warheads per submarine! As early submarine innovator Denis Papin would surely agree, that's one way to reach out and "touch the enemy."

The first ballistic-missile submarine, launched by the U.S. Navy in 1959, was named *George Washington* for the general who gave Bushnell's *Turtle* a chance to make history.

Rising from the mist like a sea creature, the nuclear-powered USS Ohio, the first of the Ohio-class subs, packs a whale of a punch in its missile system.

CHAPTER TWO

Samuel Colt
and the Revolver

During the latter part of the 1800s, in the heyday of America's Wild West, folks called the Single Action Army Model 1873 by several different names. To some, Samuel Colt's most famous revolver was known as the "Equalizer" since the popular firearm was likely to be carried by both sides in a gunfight. Others called their guns "Peacemakers," which did not quite fit since the revolvers made killing a whole lot easier. In any case, the name most people did *not* use was "Single Action Army Model 1873."

Had he still been alive in the 1870s, Colt would have been pleased. "Peacemaker" and "Equalizer" were catchy names that captured the imagination. And once that happened, Colt knew, he could sell the public just about anything.

Samuel Colt was born on July 19, 1814, on a farm near Hartford, Connecticut. Samuel's father, Christopher, owned a factory that processed silk from the cocoons of silkworms. When Samuel was

Samuel Colt (1814-1862) owed his success as much to his ability to promote himself and his guns as to the quality of the weapons themselves.

The Colt Single Action Army Model 1873, with six shots in its revolving cylinder and a solid frame, is Colt's most famous gun and the firearm credited with "winning the West." This Single Action Army revolver was the 10,588th manufactured.

10, he began helping his father and learned to use the tools and machines in the silk plant. Christopher Colt had invented a water-operated machine to unwrap the silken cocoons, a much faster method than the traditional way of working by hand. As time went by, it became obvious that Christopher's mechanical ability had rubbed off on his son.

One of Samuel Colt's favorite pastimes was shooting. At age 10, Samuel was punished for firing an old flintlock gun on a Sunday. A few years later, he again got into trouble for target practicing, this time on school property. With his knowledge of firearms, the teenager quickly realized the biggest problem with the guns of his day was their sluggish rate of fire.

While most guns at the time were single-shot flintlocks, some multi-shot flintlocks were available. The "pepperbox" revolver, a firearm with a revolving

six-barrel cluster that resembled a pepper shaker, had been around since 1780. Another handgun, patented in 1818 by Elisha Collier of Boston, Massachusetts, relied not on a revolving cluster of barrels, but on a cylinder that housed the gunpowder and shot and spun at the base of a single barrel. Although Collier's revolver wasn't as popular as the pepperbox, the British army did purchase limited numbers for its troops stationed in India.

The flintlock firing mechanism, however, was impractical for repeating firearms. For one thing, it was slow because it fired only after the sparks traveled through the touchhole to ignite the main charge. But with the revolver, there was an additional problem involving the steel plate that the flint struck to produce sparks. After every shot, it had to be lowered into its ready position above the priming pan. Some gun designers—Collier included—tried

The pepperbox revolver could be shot six times without reloading. The six barrels bundled together gave the gun a stout look compared to the later single-barreled revolvers.

The **touchhole** was a hole near the **breech**, the closed end of a gun's barrel. It got its name because in the earliest guns the gunner touched the hole with a hot coal or lit match to ignite the main charge.

to design a mechanism that would make the plate snap downward when the cock was pulled back with the thumb. Collier, like most, failed in the attempt.

There was an alternative to the clumsy flint-lock. In 1799, Englishman Edward Howard had discovered fulminate of mercury, a sensitive chemical compound that exploded when it was struck. Alexander Forsyth, a minister from Scotland, soon took advantage of Howard's find. Forsyth was an avid bird hunter who was continuously frustrated with his flintlock musket. Every time he pulled the trigger, there would be a bright flash, then a slight delay while the flash traveled through the touchhole and ignited the main powder charge packed inside the gun's breech. The alarmed bird had usually begun to fly before the musket finally discharged.

In Howard's discovery, Forsyth recognized a way to fire faster. After thorough testing, Forsyth unveiled his "percussion" system in 1807. It relied on an inch-long apparatus—called a scent bottle because of its perfume-bottle appearance—attached to the weapon where the priming pan previously sat. Inside the bottle was powdered fulminate of mercury. Before pulling the trigger, the minister rotated the bottle to deposit some of the fulminate of mercury into the touchhole. When the trigger was pulled, the cock (or hammer, as it was now sometimes called) sprang forward and struck the powder. The impact on the fulminate sent an explosion through the touchhole to the main charge, which, to Forsyth's delight, fired almost instantaneously. The minis-ter's birds were now sitting ducks.

Forsyth's percussion system didn't last long. Joshua Shaw of Philadelphia, Pennsylvania, patented a better way to use fulminate of mercury in 1814. Shaw's percussion cap was a bit of metal shaped like a miniature top hat, in which the inventor enclosed the sensitive chemical. Shaw simply placed the cap on a nipple protruding from the touchhole, where it would be struck by the hammer.

Throughout the 1820s, gunsmiths designed weapons that relied on the new ignition system. Collier modified his own revolvers to use percussion caps—inventing, as a result, the first percussion revolver. Collier's gun, however, never caught fire with the public. It had some flaws, but the biggest reason Collier failed and eventually quit the arms business for good in 1828 was that he had no ability to sell his idea to the public. The path was now clear for Samuel Colt, a firearms enthusiast who just happened to be a natural-born salesman.

In August 1830, having decided on a life at sea, 16-year-old Samuel talked his way onto a merchant ship as an apprentice. While on shore in London, England, and Calcutta, India, Samuel likely spotted Collier revolvers for the first time. The young sailor knew a good idea when he saw one. With a few modifications, and a whole lot of salesmanship, he felt a percussion revolver just might succeed.

Samuel Colt returned to Connecticut in 1831 and quickly set to work designing an improved revolver. But he needed money to hire a gunsmith to construct a prototype—a model to test before beginning final production.

Beginning in the 1860s, inventers began to package explosive powder and shot in cardboard cartridges. Ammunition makers soon started making metal instead of cardboard cartridges. Now plastic cartridges are used.

Never one to admit such an ordinary way of conceiving an idea, Colt himself told different stories of how he came up with the design for his revolver. Watching the captain steer the ship, Colt noticed that the wheel turned and locked in place. The cylinder he would fashion for his revolvers also turned and locked in place so that five separate rounds of ammunition could be fired before reloading.

At this point, Colt the innovator took a backseat to Colt the salesman. Borrowing equipment from his father's silk factory, he rigged up a machine to make nitrous oxide, or "laughing gas." Colt then went on the road selling samples of the gas and assorted patent medicines. To add an aura of sophistication and credibility to his traveling sideshow, Colt altered the spelling of his name in advertisements. Overnight, the teenaged Samuel Colt of Hartford became the "Celebrated Dr. Coult of New York, London, and Calcutta."

Colt's outings were a huge success. Crowds were so big that he often had to give two demonstrations a night. That's especially impressive given that a whiff of Colt's product wasn't exactly cheap. At a time when a whole dinner cost about 15 cents, a sample of Dr. Coult's laughing gas set customers back anywhere from a quarter to a half-dollar. After four years, Samuel had saved enough money to finance several prototypes of his new revolver. He was now ready to apply for a patent.

Patents give inventors the exclusive right to produce, sell, and profit from their creations for a certain number of years. By February 1836, France, England, and the United States had granted Colt patent rights for his weapon. Since his U.S. patent wasn't due to expire until 1857, Colt was set to dominate the repeating-firearm market for the next 21 years. It was quite an achievement for someone who had yet to celebrate his 22nd birthday.

Despite this success, Colt still lacked enough money to build a factory. Hoping for a contract with a big enough advance to fund an arms plant, Colt boldly took his weapon to the person who could offer him the most valuable deal—President Andrew Jackson. This time, however, his slick sales pitch wasn't enough. His weapon performed poorly in government tests. To Colt's chagrin, the president turned down his revolver and chose the tried-and-true flintlock for the military.

But Colt wasn't about to quit. Before the president even made up his mind, the young gunmaker had embarked on a whirlwind of public demonstrations. By March 1836, he had secured enough money from investors to open the Patent Arms Manufacturing Company in Paterson, New Jersey. The factory's first rifles and handguns were unveiled by the end of December. Unfortunately, Colt again

Andrew Jackson (1767-1845) was the greatest military hero of the time, a veteran of the War of 1812 and numerous battles with Indians.

Colt's factory in Paterson, New Jersey, in 1840. It was a modern, efficient facility, but sales suffered. Colt's early guns were not always reliable and the government was hesitant to buy the firearms.

ran smack into the same obstacle that had brought down Elisha Collier—a lack of public and military interest in the new design.

There were several reasons for the less-than-dazzling response. Typical of any new weapon, Colt's revolvers had several bugs that could only be worked out over time. Cylinders and barrels occasionally burst, while percussion caps sometimes splintered and flew into the firer's face. Few people were willing to trade their trusted flintlocks for Colt's unfamiliar—and possibly dangerous—revolver. An even bigger problem for Colt proved to be a lack of any major military conflicts. With no fighting going on, fewer people needed multi-firing weapons.

Colt did manage to sell a few of his revolvers to U.S. military units fighting the Seminole Indians in Florida—but only because he brought a batch of weapons into the swamps and sold them to individual officers. Overall, despite Colt's enthusiastic courting of government officials and other prospective customers, sales continued to slide. In 1842, Colt's Paterson arms plant was forced to close.

The young innovator, like Collier before him, suddenly found himself out of the arms business. But that's where the similarities ended. Determined to make his fortune with some type of weapon, Colt designed an underwater mine activated by electricity.

The electrically detonated mines were making waves by 1845 and seemed on the verge of bringing Colt fame and fortune. But war loomed with Mexico over Texas and every aspiring arms merchant took notice. Colt turned back to his revolver.

The electric cable Colt designed for his mines could also be used to send electric telegraph messages. Colt used it to send the first successful underwater telegraph message across New York City's harbor.

THE BREAKTHROUGH

Unfortunately, when war broke out between Mexico and the United States in 1846, Colt wasn't ready. To begin with, he was unable to find any of the old Paterson weapons to use as models for production. Even worse, Colt had no factory and no money to start one. Little did he know, these delays would end up working to his advantage.

While Colt was scrounging for firearms and money, he met his biggest fan in Samuel Hamilton Walker of the military unit known as the Texas Rangers. Before he had enlisted in the elite unit, Walker had been in Florida fighting Seminoles. There he had come across some of the pistols that Colt had sold to the soldiers stationed in Florida. Although the weapons had a few problems, Walker developed a fondness for the quick-firing Colts.

Walker joined the Texas Rangers in 1842 and was pleased to find Colt guns again. Between 1839 and 1841, Texas had acquired several hundred revolvers from Colt's Paterson plant. These weapons were soon credited with a stunning battle victory.

"In the Summer of 1844," wrote Walker in a letter to Colt a few years later, "15 men fought about 80 Comanche Indians, boldly attacking them upon their own ground, killing & wounding about half their number." Regarded as vastly superior horse soldiers by the Texans, the Comanches nonetheless fell that day to Walker and the Rangers, who were armed with Colt revolvers. Walker became convinced that Colt's gun was the weapon of the future.

When Walker joined the U.S. Army shortly after the war with Mexico began, he was given his own command. Not surprisingly, he wanted quick-firing Colts for his soldiers. But the ex-Ranger did not want the older Paterson models that often malfunctioned at the worst possible moments.

Walker wrote to Colt, and the two began a very profitable relationship. They designed a new pistol based on Walker's specifications. A trigger guard prevented catching the trigger on a holster or an article of clothing. To simplify loading, a fold-down ramming lever was attached to the underside of the Walker-Colt. This was important, since metal cartridges had not yet been invented. Instead, paper cartridges filled with powder and shot, or just the powder and shot alone, were used. Both had to be rammed into each chamber of the revolver's cylinder.

The pair hammered out other imperfections in the old Patersons and added a sixth shot to the original five-shot cylinder. The Walker-Colt firearm was safer and more reliable than its predecessors. Since Walker wanted the gun to be useful as a club if a soldier ran out of ammunition, it was also the biggest Colt revolver ever made—15 inches long and a whopping 4.9 pounds.

As a result of Walker's lobbying, the secretary of war ordered 1,000 Walker-Colts in December 1846. Colt sent a finely engraved set of pistols to the commander of American forces in northern Mexico, future president Zachary Taylor, before the weapons were inspected in May 1847. The revolvers passed muster. Colt finally had his government contract.

Samuel Hamilton Walker (1817-1847) died on the heels of the Walker-Colt's success. Proof that old weapons were still deadly, Walker was killed in the Mexican War by the thrust of a lance.

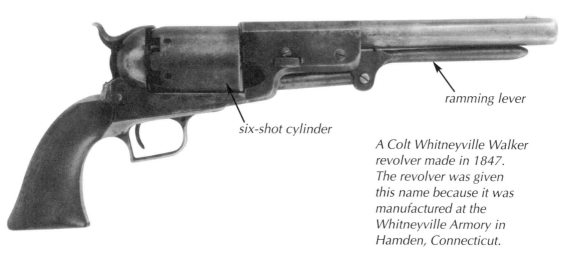

six-shot cylinder

ramming lever

A Colt Whitneyville Walker revolver made in 1847. The revolver was given this name because it was manufactured at the Whitneyville Armory in Hamden, Connecticut.

THE RESULT

Colt's fortune was assured following the success in Mexico of the Walker-Colt. Other events, like the California gold rush of 1849, the Crimean War in Russia (1853-1856), and the American Civil War (1861-1865), continued to fuel demand for deadly, quick-firing weapons. And as Americans headed westward across the Great Plains and beyond, they brought along handy Colt revolvers for protection. Boosted by the fact that legendary gunfighters such as "Wild Bill" Hickok and "Buffalo Bill" Cody swore by the weapons, a sort of frontier spirit started to surround the six-shooters.

Colt's name became synonymous with the word "revolver." While he had a knack for taking the good ideas of others and refining them into successful weapons, Colt owed his fame and fortune to

"Buffalo Bill" Cody (1846-1917) opened a hugely popular and long-running extravaganza, "Buffalo Bill's Wild West Show," in 1883.

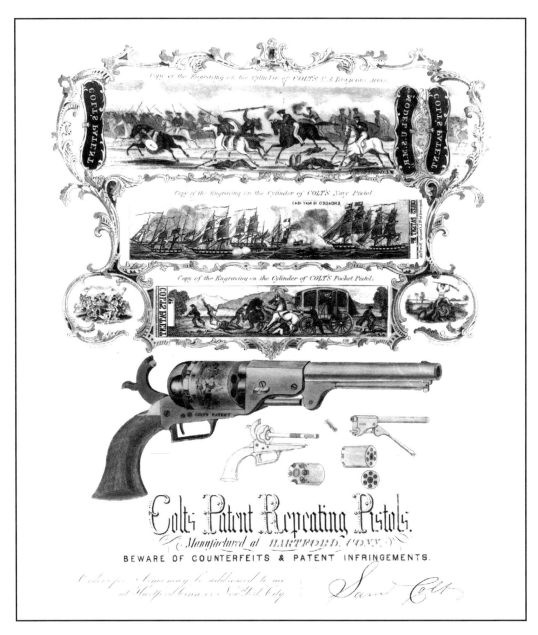

This advertisement shows scenes decorating the cylinders of several Colt firearms. The top image portrays the Texas Rangers fighting Comanche Indians; the center scene is a naval battle; and a stagecoach is defended against highwaymen in the bottom illustration.

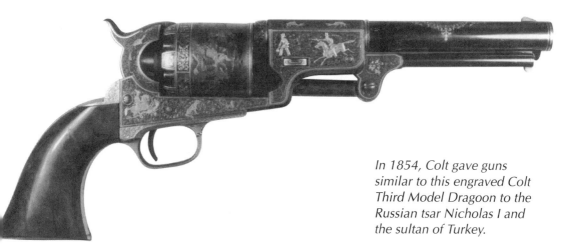

In 1854, Colt gave guns similar to this engraved Colt Third Model Dragoon to the Russian tsar Nicholas I and the sultan of Turkey.

his ability to sell his creations. Specially engraved pistols given as gifts, elaborate public demonstrations, and expensive parties for government officials were all important parts of his success. By the time Samuel Colt died on January 10, 1862, he had amassed a great fortune and his arms factory was the largest privately owned armory in the world.

Over the years, Colt guns have lost none of their appeal. The company makes some of the most widely used firearms by police and the military, including the M-16 assault rifle. One-of-a-kind Colt guns honor important events from wedding anniversaries to the American bicentennial. Special edition firearms commemorate people from the heroes of the Wild West to nearly every president of the United States. In this way, Samuel Colt's guns have woven their way into American history and culture.

CHAPTER THREE

John Ericsson
and the Battleship

It was 10:00 A.M. on January 30, 1862, and John Ericsson stood shivering atop his newest invention, the ironclad *Monitor*. In moments, the vessel would slide down its launching ramp and into the icy water of New York City's East River. While the Civil War raged further south, the only battles Ericsson had been fighting were those against the navies of the world to get his strange ship built.

Bracing himself, the inventor signaled the workers to remove the blocks holding the *Monitor* back. With a groan, the iron hulk lurched backward, then quickly picked up speed before crashing rear—or stern—first into the river. Despite the predictions of some of the most experienced officers in the U.S. Navy, Ericsson's ship didn't go straight to the bottom. Instead, the nearly submerged *Monitor* rocked gently on the waves—just like the freshly cut timber Ericsson remembered floating in the lakes of his native Sweden.

John Ericsson (1803-1889) faced years of rejection of his revolutionary ship design before he convinced one of the world's weakest navies to give him a chance.

Formerly the USS *Merrimac,* the Confederate ship was renamed the *Virginia* after being captured by Confederate forces and rebuilt.

Ericsson smiled and waved his hat. His radically new ship had won its first fight. But 300 or so miles to the south, in Norfolk, Virginia, the Confederate navy was hastily finishing its own ironclad, the *Virginia.* Ericsson knew the two would soon meet in battle. While few people at the time were willing to bet on his outgunned ship—some even called it an "iron coffin"—Ericsson wasn't the least bit worried.

John Ericsson was born on July 31, 1803, in Långbanshyttan, Sweden. Even as a young boy, he was designing successful machines. In 1808, five-year-old John melted down several of his mother's silver spoons and stripped the family's watches and clocks to get the necessary parts to build a miniature windmill. Despite the damage, John's father, Olof, admired the boy's creativity and cultivated his son's interest in science and technology.

In 1811, Olof was hired to help the Mechanical Corps of the Swedish navy—which built bridges, dams, and the sort—construct a great canal that would divide the whole country of Sweden. John spent his spare time at the work site learning how to use the tools and heavy machinery. When John was barely in his teens, the project's chief engineer noticed the young man's talent and appointed him to the corps. Advancing quickly, by 1819 the 16-year-old was overseeing the work of 600 men.

Olof had been dead for a year by that time. To make ends meet, John's mother, Brita, rented rooms to engineers from the job site. Ericsson loved the talk of steam engines and other machines that filled the house. He decided to enlist in a special engineering unit of the Swedish army. One of his jobs was to design and build steam engines for excavation and drainage of marshy land.

Ericsson designed several different types of engines over the next six years, including a wood-burning model that used hot air instead of steam to drive its internal pistons. In May 1826, the 22-year-old took his "flame engine" to London, England, with hopes of making his fortune. Unfortunately, at the trial he was forced to substitute hotter-burning coal for the wood shavings the engine used. The engine melted away before his eyes.

Luckily, Ericsson found an investor who was willing to bankroll his inventions. One product of the partnership was a steam-powered fire engine that pumped more water than older hand-operated models. Ericsson confidently approached London's fire officials with the invention, only to be turned away when they refused to part with their old, tried-and-true hand pumps. It would not be the last time Ericsson would have his hopes dashed by people afraid to embrace new technology.

If Ericsson thought he'd had a tough time selling improvements to London firefighters, he was in for a real shock from England's conservative admirals. Since October 1805, when the British fleet had annihilated the French fleet at the Battle of Trafalgar, the Royal Navy had reigned supreme. Still, Ericsson noticed, two recent developments were on the verge of rendering every ship in the mighty British fleet obsolete.

Ericsson became expert in artillery and shooting while in the Swedish army.

The first innovation was steam power. Since 1707, when Denis Papin of Germany demonstrated the first working steamboat, the *Retort*, steam power seemed destined to replace sails on all ships one day. Steam engines and navy ships were finally combined in 1814, when American Robert Fulton launched the first steam-powered warship.

While the idea had yet to catch on 12 years later, it was obvious to Ericsson that steam would free sea captains from their dependence on the wind. Still, navies shunned steam propulsion, mainly because paddle wheels were at the time the only way to push steamships through the water. Even a poor marksman could hit a giant paddle wheel—and the equally exposed engine that turned it.

The other development was still in the experimental stage, but Ericsson firmly believed it would

The paddle wheel in Fulton's steam warship, Fulton the First, *was hidden within the ship so it wouldn't be as vulnerable to attack. Fulton hoped the ship would break England's blockade of New London, Connecticut, but the War of 1812 was over before it was completed.*

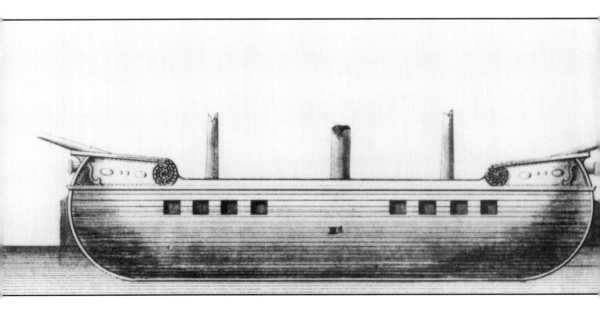

devastate wooden navies once it was widely introduced. Invented in 1822 by Henri-Joseph Paixhans of France, the artillery shell was a gunpowder-packed iron round that blew apart once embedded in a vessel's wooden hull. Ships that didn't sink outright from the gaping hole would burn to a crisp.

Realizing that shell guns and steam engines spelled doom for the world's existing navies, Ericsson suggested to British naval officials that they build only iron warships propelled by steam. The navy scoffed at his idea.

Iron ships were feasible, the officials agreed; indeed, a number of iron merchant vessels were already traveling the oceans. But they were thin-skinned vessels, not heavily armored ships of war. The problem, the admirals argued, was that steam engines already used a lot of fuel to turn their huge paddle wheels. Adding enough armor to protect against shell guns would add so much weight that engines would need to consume more coal than a warship could carry on a long voyage. Besides, the paddle wheels would never survive the first exchange of gunfire.

The admirals were right, admitted Ericsson. But he was also right. Steam and shells were the future, and any navy that refused to accept that simple fact would one day suffer extinction. While Ericsson continued to design other machines, including a railroad locomotive that set a speed record in 1829, he was obsessed with the possibility of inventing an "impregnable fighting machine" like the type he had proposed to the English admirals.

A screw propeller, now generally called a propeller

The screw propeller's method of moving water goes back to the Archimedes screw, a device invented by Greek mathematician Archimedes in the third century B.C. By turning his screw, it was possible to lift water out of streams. In 1752, another mathematician, Daniel Bernoulli, theorized that a similar contraption could be used to propel boats.

Since autumn 1853, Russia had been battling the Ottoman Empire in the Crimean War. The European nations France and Great Britain declared war on Russia and joined the fray in March 1854.

THE BREAKTHROUGH

Step number one for Ericsson was designing a method of propulsion that was more efficient and less vulnerable than the paddle wheel. To this end, he patented the first practical screw propeller in 1836. Ericsson's device, which has become standard on most watercraft in use today, was much easier for a steam engine to turn than a paddle wheel. Also, because it rests near the bottom of a ship, a propeller is virtually invulnerable to enemy gunfire. Amazingly, the British admirals refused to embrace even this technology. The disgusted inventor packed his bags and moved to the United States in 1839.

Better luck awaited him there. The U.S. Navy backed Ericsson's design of a propeller-driven warship. When the USS *Princeton* was launched in 1843, it carried both its propeller and its steam engines beneath the waterline, making it the first ship with its entire propulsion system beyond reach of enemy fire. Still, it was a wooden ship fully rigged with masts and sails. His invulnerable ship, Ericsson had finally learned, would have to be put together one small step at a time.

With the outbreak of Europe's Crimean War in 1853, the time seemed right for new ideas. Ericsson approached France in September 1854, with designs for his indestructible vessel in hand. While the naval leaders acknowledged the inferiority of wooden ships, they weren't too thrilled with the other features of Ericsson's proposed ironclad. For one thing, to reduce the amount of heavy armor,

Ericsson planned to place most of his ship beneath the water and out of harm's way. Even more bizarre, the ship had only one gun, which would be mounted in a turret atop the deck. The admirals laughed at the idea of a half-sunken warship steaming into battle armed with a single cannon! Needless to say, they rejected Ericsson's proposal. Frustrated again, the innovator returned to the United States.

Five years later, in 1859, the French finally made an effort to modernize and built the first ironclad. *La Gloire*, however, was nothing more than a traditional sailing ship overlaid with iron plates. England launched the *Warrior* the next year, but it was not much better. Although it had an iron body, its skeleton was still made of oak. The *Warrior* also sported sails for propulsion and 50 guns along its sides for firepower—the same type of ship that had dominated the oceans for the past 300 years! The world's top navies, clinging to the past, were not yet ready for Ericsson's futuristic design.

It was one of the world's weakest navies that finally took the chance. When the Civil War broke out in 1861, the United States had the second greatest merchant fleet in the world. Its navy, on the other hand, was abysmal. When word filtered northward that the Confederates had converted a captured wooden sailing ship—the *Merrimac*—into an ironclad named the *Virginia*, most leaders in the federal capital panicked. Calls went out for inventors to submit proposals for armored ships. Out of 17 designs, it was Ericsson's plan for a turreted vessel that won the government contract.

THE RESULT

When the USS *Monitor* was launched in January 1862 under the command of John Worden, Ericsson believed he was on the verge of achieving his 36-year-old dream of building a vessel immune to all enemy obstacles. Little more than a month later, on March 9, 1862, the *Monitor* faced the test of battle. In an engagement that lasted four hours, Ericsson's ironclad slugged it out with the *Virginia*. It was not only the world's first battle between iron-armored ships, but also one of the earliest all-steamship fights.

The stage had been set the day earlier, when the Confederate ironclad had utterly destroyed the Union ships *Cumberland* and *Congress*, two warships straight out of the past. That battle was the death

This lithograph of the famous battle between the Monitor *(low in the water in front) and the* Virginia *(with smokestack) has a glaring inaccuracy: it includes the* Cumberland *(at left) and the* Congress *(behind the* Virginia*), both of which the* Virginia *had sunk the day before!*

knell for wooden navies. But how would the rebel ship stand up to the *Monitor*?

Just fine, as it turned out. The ironclads punished each other with hours of artillery fire, often at ranges of not more than a few yards, but neither seemed capable of doing much harm to the other. In fact, according to a *Virginia* crew member, shots bounced off the two vessels "with no more effect than so many pebble stones thrown by a child." When the battle ended and the vessels withdrew, many casual observers considered the fight a draw.

But experienced sailors knew better. Like all other ships, the *Virginia* had to shift its entire position to fire its guns, which were fixed in place mainly

Some of the 58 crew members of the Monitor *wait for lunch on deck beside the turret, a revolving gun platform surrounded by a thick iron wall.*

Whereas we had available for immediate purposes one hundred and forty-nine first-class war-ships, we have now two, these two being the *Warrior* and her sister *Ironside*. There is not now a ship in the English navy apart from these two that it would not be madness to trust to an engagement with that little *Monitor*.
　　　　　—London *Times*

The original Monitor *went down in a storm at sea later in 1862, but more "monitors" were quickly built.*

along its sides. In contrast, the *Monitor*'s revolving turret could swing around in seconds, allowing its two big cannons to fire from any position relative to the enemy. Had the *Monitor*'s cannons been loaded with better quality ammunition, they certainly would have destroyed the *Virginia*. With the advantages of a revolving turret obvious to all, Ericsson's unique vessel—ridiculed before the fight as a "cheese box on a raft"—became the basis for all future battleships.

The U.S. Navy quickly ordered additional "monitors," as this class of ships came to be known. Other nations ceased constructing wooden ships and concentrated instead on developing their own iron-clads. By 1870, the most heavily armored and armed war vessels began to take on the name "battleship."

By the start of World War I in 1914, battleships looked considerably different than the *Monitor*. Still, Great Britain's *Dreadnought*, the most powerful ship ever constructed when it was launched in 1906, was an unmistakable descendant of Ericsson's ironclad. With 10 guns inside five revolving turrets, the *Dreadnought* could fire 6,800 pounds of high-explosive rounds at once—almost 20 times the firepower of its Civil War ancestor! Battleships only grew bigger. Japan's World War II battleships *Yamato* and *Musashi* still rank as the biggest ever built. Each had nine turreted cannons able to fire shells weighing 3,200 pounds apiece for distances up to 20 miles.

Spurred by the threat of war with Germany, the British rushed to build the Dreadnought, *which combined awesome firepower with armor almost a foot thick. Like the* Monitor, *the* Dreadnought *became the name for a whole new class of battleships.*

The Yamato *battleship of Japan, equipped with 18-inch guns, was the largest warship ever built, but it was nevertheless vulnerable to the world's new air forces.*

The first major missile duel between surface ships happened in the Persian Gulf on April 18, 1988, when the USS *Strauss* used an Exocet missile with a 364-pound warhead to sink the Iranian vessel *Sahand.*

The Second World War (1939-1945) was the heyday of the big-gun battleship. But weapons emerged that surpassed long-range cannons in effectiveness and accuracy. Both the *Yamato* and *Musashi,* for instance, were sunk during the war by torpedoes and bombs delivered not by ships, but by airplanes based on a new kind of ship called an aircraft carrier.

The newly invented missile was another weapon that would ultimately replace the warship's big naval gun. Tomahawk cruise missiles launched from U.S. ships during the Persian Gulf War of 1991 caused destruction no gun could match. A direct descendant of the jet-propelled V-1 "buzz bomb" developed by the Germans during World War II, the Tomahawk can deliver its warhead (including nuclear warheads) to within feet of any target up to

1,550 miles away. And when ships want to destroy other ships, they can always turn to the French radar-guided sea-skimming Exocet missile. The 1,800-pound weapon can track and destroy surface craft more than 43 miles from its point of fire.

Today, there are no more battleships, their missions being performed either by aircraft carriers or missile-firing ships. As for John Ericsson, he would live only to see the rise in the popularity of his weapon, not its decline. He died at the age of 85 on March 8, 1889, one day shy of the anniversary of the Civil War victory of his remarkable invention.

The USS Nimitz, one of the U.S. Navy's premier aircraft carriers, is 1,100 feet long, holds about 6,000 people, and can be used by up to 80 aircraft at a time.

CHAPTER FOUR

Robert Whitehead and the Torpedo

It came to Robert Whitehead one sleepless night in late 1868—the long-sought secret to his new weapon. The self-propelled torpedo would revolutionize naval warfare, the inventor believed, enabling the smallest torpedo-armed vessels to sink even the biggest ironclads. But what kept Whitehead up that night was what would happen to him as a result. As he reached for his notebook to sketch the image, he was sure his secret would transform him into a very wealthy—and world-famous—inventor.

From the day of his birth in Bolton, England, on January 3, 1823, Robert was surrounded by mechanical inventions. His mother's family designed and built various machines, like steam engines, mill machinery, and hydraulic—or water-operated—presses. James, his father, ran a textile business when Robert was born, then switched to beer brewing a dozen years later. As a child, Robert played among the various engines, presses, and brewing pumps.

Robert Whitehead (1823-1905) had bad experiences with people stealing his ideas, so when he hit upon the solution to creating a workable torpedo, he called it "the secret" and revealed it only to his most trusted associates.

In 1839, Robert was hired by one of his uncles, who ran an engineering firm. The teenager worked daily with steam engines and other machinery and became fascinated with their operation. When his uncle took a position managing a shipyard in France in the mid-1840s, he offered Robert a job designing steam engines. The ambitious Whitehead accepted. He left England with his new bride, Frances Maria.

But Whitehead soon grew restless working under his uncle's wing. In 1847, he and Frances moved to Milan in northern Italy, where Whitehead hoped to make his fortune designing machinery for the silk-weaving industry. It was not long before he was reaping substantial profits from the royalties factory owners paid to use his patented inventions.

All that soon changed. Throughout the countryside in 1848, Italians were rising up to fight for independence from the Austrian Empire. After five days of bloody fighting in March, victorious Italian nationalists captured Milan. The new government canceled all patents previously issued by the "foreign" government in Vienna. As part of the patent process, inventors reveal their designs. When Whitehead lost his patent protection, the secrets behind his inventions became public knowledge. No longer could Whitehead earn money from his designs. The disgusted inventor vowed never again to patent anything or reveal his secrets to anyone.

Austria regained its power quickly, but the damage to Whitehead's work was done. Frances was now expecting a child, so Robert decided to move his family somewhere more stable. For a brief time before he left, local Austrian officials paid him to design steam-operated pumps for the drainage of some nearby marshy land. After successfully draining the marsh, Whitehead accepted a job as technical director of a marine-engine plant located in a safer region of Austrian-controlled Italy. For the next seven years, Whitehead's reputation as an innovative steam-engine designer steadily grew.

In 1856, 33-year-old Whitehead accepted a position managing a nearby shipyard. Although he could not have known it then, the new job would lead directly to his yearned-for fame and fortune.

Once again, it was the Italian nationalists who nudged Whitehead toward his destiny. In 1859, they teamed up with France to capture an Austrian province they claimed as their own. Then they set their sights on the rest of Austrian-controlled Italy. When France launched *La Gloire*, the world's first ironclad warship, in 1859, the worried Austrians made a contract with Whitehead's employer to build a similar armed vessel. As manager of the shipyard, it was Whitehead's responsibility to oversee the design and construction of the ironclad. As he worked on that project and others over the course of the next five years, Whitehead gained valuable insights into the weaknesses of all armored ships—especially their vulnerability to blows beneath the waterline, where their armor was thinnest.

In 1864, Whitehead was visited at the shipyard by Giovanni de Luppis, a retired Austrian sailor. The old man hoped for some technical advice from the well-known engineer. De Luppis had in tow a small wooden boat roughly two feet long, filled with gunpowder and fitted with a tiny motorized propeller. He envisioned the device skimming along the surface and exploding against the side of an enemy ship. Problem was, the thing didn't work. Whitehead, always eager to tinker with any machine, agreed to look at de Luppis's novel contraption.

Whitehead had no better luck than de Luppis. Because of its clockwork engine, the boat had little speed and even less range. Worse, it had to be steered by manipulating wires attached to its rudder—kind of like flying a kite. Even if the operator (who would be riding in a nearby boat) managed to guide de Luppis's floating bomb close to the enemy, observant sailors on the target vessel would likely destroy the bomb—along with its operator—long before it could cause damage. Disappointed that Whitehead couldn't help him, de Luppis gathered up his boat and left, apparently never giving the device a second thought.

Giovanni de Luppis called his proposed weapon Der Küstenbrander, *or the coastal fireship.*

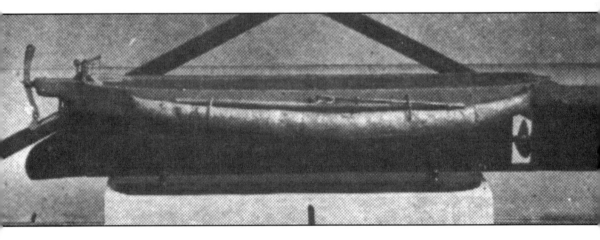

Whitehead, in contrast, became obsessed with the idea. He knew from working on the Austrian ironclad that a bomb could destroy an armored ship if it hit the right spot. Due to an ironclad's thin armor beneath the waterline, a subsurface impact would cause a lot more damage than a surface strike. Also, if the bomb's path to the enemy lay beneath the surface, enemy sailors would not be able to defend against it. They would never see it coming. The bomb Whitehead envisioned thus had to be self-guided and self-propelled. It would be a stealthy underwater killer.

Actually, Whitehead's idea of blowing up ships from beneath the water was nothing new. Almost a century earlier, during the American Revolution, colonist David Bushnell had developed an underwater explosive device that could destroy British ships as they lay at anchor. Bushnell's bomb, however, was not self-propelled or self-guided. Instead, it had to be attached to the ships almost by hand.

Another naval innovator had a better idea. Robert Fulton, best known for introducing a practical steamboat in 1807, contributed much to the advancement of undersea warfare. In the late 1790s and early 1800s, Fulton improved on Bushnell's bomb by anchoring it to the ocean floor so that it floated just below the surface. Armed with a contact fuse, Fulton's weapon was set to destroy any boat that touched it. It was Fulton who started calling all of his explosive devices "torpedoes" after a type of stinging fish. The name was appropriate, and it stuck.

The U.S. Postal Service honored Robert Fulton for his contributions with a stamp commemorating the 200th anniversary of his birth.

In Fulton's drawing, the underwater mines floated out of sight beneath the surface until struck by an enemy ship, at which point they would explode (see ship at left).

The next innovator to take up torpedoes was Samuel Colt, who later won fame for his revolver. In 1842, he demonstrated an electrically detonated anchored mine in New York City's harbor. To blow up the mine, Colt sent an electric charge through a cable running under the water to the bomb.

During the American Civil War 20 years later, torpedoes destroyed many ships on both sides. One model attached to a long pole—or spar—was used in the first successful submarine attack in history. Such a mission, however, was often as dangerous for the attacker as for the victim because the vessel delivering the spar torpedo had to approach so close to its intended target.

But all that was ancient history, as far as Robert Whitehead was concerned. For the next two years, he dove into the design and construction of what would be a radically new weapon. There was much to do, since nearly everything about the undersea missile, including guidance and propulsion systems, had to be designed from scratch.

Finally, in December 1866, a rough prototype was ready for testing. Just six months earlier, the Austrian ironclad whose construction Whitehead had supervised won an impressive victory over similar Italian vessels. The inventor took advantage of his new celebrity to secure a test date with Austrian naval officials. With a little luck, the admirals would look favorably on his strange-looking device.

Whitehead's design was ingenious. Like fins on a fish, closely cropped fins on both sides of the torpedo stabilized the weapon as it glided beneath the surface. The torpedo was equally impressive inside. Whitehead had invented an engine fueled by compressed air that was far more powerful than de Luppis's wimpy clockwork model. And because there was no bulky boiler, Whitehead's engine was tiny compared with a steam engine of equal power.

Whitehead's torpedo worked reasonably well, except for one major deficiency that continued to dog the missile for the next two years—an inability to remain at a constant depth. All too often, it either surfaced or dove to the bottom.

As Whitehead searched for an answer to the depth problem, he worked on other parts of his weapon system. He built the first underwater launch tube, a device that ensured his torpedo would remain hidden below the waterline from the moment it was fired. Still, his torpedo failed in trial after trial. Without depth control, Whitehead's torpedo would only destroy itself. So much for fame and fortune.

Whitehead's original torpedo weighed about 300 pounds and was 11 feet, 7 inches long and 14 inches in diameter at its widest point. A dynamite warhead was packed in its nose.

THE BREAKTHROUGH

One night in October 1868, after a particularly depressing test saw his torpedo hit its mark only 8 of 54 times, Whitehead lay in bed, too upset to sleep. Once again, the missile had launched correctly, kept a constant speed, and maintained a fairly straight course from side to side. But the weapon failed to maintain its proper depth of 12 feet. Whitehead knew there had to be some way for the torpedo to monitor and maintain its depth, but how? For all his creativity, he was stumped.

Then it hit him. Water pressure increases with depth. Any workable depth-finding device would have to measure the pressure exerted by the water. Then that information had to be relayed to the elevator flaps attached to the torpedo's tail end.

Whitehead hopped out of bed and began sketching. What he ended up with was a disc-shaped valve suspended within a "balance chamber" inside the torpedo. The valve would be rigged to the rudder by a system of levers. As the weapon glided beneath the surface, the valve would constantly make slight depth corrections until the torpedo struck its target. Having come up with the device that would finally make his weapon work, Whitehead had no trouble naming it. He called it "the secret" and refused to reveal its true design to government or military officials.

Tests for the Austrian navy resumed, and the improved torpedo was an immediate success. So accurate was the new depth-regulating mechanism

Elevator flaps are surfaces that can be tilted up or down to control vertical movement. Horizontal movement is guided by shifting the **rudder** side to side.

The balance chamber that contained "the secret" of the Whitehead torpedo. This method of controlling depth, which was accurate within six inches, was used until the end of World War II.

that the torpedo consistently struck its intended target. Whitehead had finally demonstrated a reliable weapon powerful enough to sink anything afloat. The Austrians, now convinced of the weapon's power, placed their orders.

Whitehead next targeted Britain's Royal Navy. In April 1871, he inked a deal with the English that gave them the right to build the weapon in their own factories. The other navies of the world, already outclassed by the powerful British fleet, had to scramble if they hoped not to fall further behind. The French were the first, adopting the torpedo in 1872. A year later, Germany and Italy—which had finally won its independence from Austria in 1866— placed their orders. By 1877, Russia, Turkey, Greece, Portugal, Belgium, Denmark, and Chile had bought the weapon as well.

As Whitehead had envisioned, the torpedo was beginning to change the world's navies. Now even one small boat packing "Whiteheads" could spell doom for an unsuspecting ironclad. Then, in 1885, Thorsten Nordenfeldt introduced a totally new type of torpedo boat—one that could sneak up on its target completely submerged. This was the beginning of a still-successful marriage between the submarine and the self-propelled torpedo.

By that time, Whitehead's weapon had finally proven itself in combat. On January 25, 1878, a direct hit by two Russian Whitehead torpedoes sent a Turkish steamship to the bottom of the Black Sea in less than two minutes. The superiority of the Whitehead torpedoes was clear. The Russians had also attacked several times with spar torpedoes, only

The torpedo was first fired in action (without hitting the enemy) on May 20, 1877, by the British ship Shah *(left) against the ironclad* Huascar, *sailed by a Peruvian pirate and revolutionary.*

The Chilean armored sailing ship Blanco Encalada, *sunk by rebels firing Whitehead torpedoes on April 23, 1891, was the first ironclad to be destroyed by a torpedo.*

A **gyroscope** is a wheel that rotates on an axis, much like a spinning top. When a gyroscope is suspended within a set of rings, its spinning motion will always keep it pointed in its original direction, no matter how much the rings shift. This characteristic made it possible to use a gyroscope to maintain the torpedo's accuracy.

to have one of their torpedo boats almost destroyed in the explosion that followed. It paid to be as far from the target as possible when attacking, and only a self-propelled torpedo gave that option.

Still, the torpedo had a tendency to deviate slightly from its intended target. No navies complained, and sales didn't suffer, but Whitehead knew he could do better. In 1895, he found he could use the stabilizing effects of another recent innovation—the gyroscope. He inserted one of the devices into his weapon with the gyroscope's axis running along the length of the torpedo. Whitehead then devised a way for the gyroscope to activate the missile's rudder. Once he put the gyroscope in motion, both its axis and the nose of the torpedo remained set on course.

THE RESULT

Even before the death of Robert Whitehead on November 14, 1905, torpedoes had become the dominant naval weapon. In the Russo-Japanese War (1904-1905) that had ended just five months before Whitehead died, Japan wielded its torpedo boats with ruthless effectiveness against the Russian navy, sinking two battleships and several other armored vessels at the Battle of Tsushima.

Most early submarine designers in this period followed Nordenfeldt's practice of including the Whitehead torpedo as the sub's main weapon. One of them, Irish-born John P. Holland, pioneered submarine development after moving to the United States in 1873. He became the victor of the race to sell the U.S. Navy its first submarine in 1900.

The first of Germany's *Unterseeboten*—undersea boats—the *U-1*, was finished in December 1906.

When Germany unleashed its fleet of U-boats in 1914, the Allied forces in World War I panicked at the underwater menace—not least because the submarines torpedoed commercial vessels as well as warships.

The German G7 torpedo of World War I could potentially hit a target at a distance of over 3.5 miles, but its accuracy was poor. Of 5,000 torpedoes launched, only 2,000 found their marks.

The Asroc, like most torpedoes today, is powered with an electric motor.

The Germans' combination of submarine and torpedo technology came close to winning the First World War for the German navy in 1917. The Allies were terror-stricken by the invisible enemy.

Torpedoes have continued to evolve. By World War I, German models weighed almost 2,500 pounds and cruised at speeds close to 40 miles per hour. Their range was in excess of 3.5 miles. While the British torpedoes of the Second World War were about the same size and only 5 miles per hour faster than the German version, they could strike down enemy vessels 8.5 miles away.

Today, torpedoes like Subroc (a submarine-launched solid-fuel rocket) can pack a nuclear punch. Designed to obliterate submarines that fire ballistic missiles, Subroc is launched from the submarine as a rocket that shoots to the surface. Once free of the water, the weapon flies to a predetermined spot above the target sub. A nuclear warhead separates from the missile and dives beneath the water until it's just over the enemy. Then it explodes and decimates the enemy sub.

There are other types of torpedo-rocket combinations as well. Once launched by either a surface ship or an airplane, weapons like Asroc (anti-sub rocket) fly through the air until they are over their target. The torpedo then separates, dives, and homes in on its prey by "listening" to the sound the doomed enemy sub makes. Like Subroc, Asroc can also carry a nuclear warhead. The primitive explosives of Bushnell, Fulton, and even Whitehead have certainly come a long way.

Robert Whitehead knew that his weapon would transform warfare by making any ship—including ironclads—vulnerable to an enemy. The weapon transformed him, as well. He became a very rich and famous man. As the inscription on his tombstone reads, "His fame was in all nations 'round about." Although Whitehead's fame did not actually last long, for many years torpedoes were called "Whiteheads"—even after their inventor was, in the end, largely forgotten and neglected by history.

A half-ton Asroc launched by a ship can travel over six miles before its torpedo is released to drop on its enemy target.

CHAPTER FIVE

Hiram Maxim
and the Automatic Machine Gun

Hiram Maxim came up with the idea for the world's first automatic machine gun while target practicing with a heavy single-shot rifle in 1882. The vision didn't just pop into his head in a flash of inspiration—it hit him square in the shoulder!

You see, all firearms produce a recoil when they're fired. The reason is best explained in Isaac Newton's Third Law of Motion: For every action there is an equal and opposite reaction. In Maxim's case, the action was the explosive force of the gunpowder charge pushing the bullet towards the open end of the barrel. That caused a reaction—the recoil—in the opposite direction. After a few shots, the recoil turned Maxim's shoulder black and blue. Instead of wasting the recoil energy of the shots, Maxim reasoned, why not harness it and use it to operate the weapon?

There was only one problem. Gun experts did not believe that a gun's recoil could power it through

Hiram Maxim (1840-1916) made a name for himself in electrical engineering and aviation as well as in weaponry, installing some of the first electric lights and building what was in 1894 the largest and most powerful (though unsuccessful) airplane in the world.

all the stages of firing. Even the Gatling gun—the most advanced rapid-fire gun at the time—depended on the muscle power of its operator to turn a crank. A prominent maker of rifle barrels tried to dissuade Maxim, bluntly telling him that he didn't "stand a ghost of a chance."

Maxim disagreed. "I am," he replied, "a totally different mechanic from any you have ever seen before, a different breed." Today, when we think of mechanics, we think of cars. But in the days before automobiles, "mechanic" meant anyone expert in the design, construction, or operation of any type of tool or machine. Maxim, who had spent his whole life designing and refining machines, tools, and other gadgets, believed that he could create a workable machine gun. He was right.

The Gatling gun was both mobile and powerful, with 6 to 10 barrels firing up to 1,200 rounds per minute in later models.

The inventor of one of the deadliest weapons in history was born in the small town of Sangerville, Maine, on February 5, 1840. Even as a boy, Hiram Stevens Maxim was a good shot with his musket and often hunted bear with his brother, Leander. In 1852, Hiram's knack for building mechanical devices first became apparent. When he could not afford a chronometer, a highly accurate timepiece that he needed for some scientific experiments, young Hiram built his own. It worked perfectly.

By mid-1854, 14-year-old Hiram was working as an apprentice for a carriage-maker. The teenager was soon sketching improvements for the shop's tools and the various parts used in the carriages. When he wasn't drawing, he was gaining extensive experience with the machinery used in the shop.

After four years in the carriage business, Maxim decided to put his knowledge of machines to work for himself. He built a gristmill to grind grain for area farmers. The business attracted not only grain growers, but also a great many mice. Maxim devised a simple mousetrap that worked well enough, but after catching a mouse, it had to be reset. So the inventor discarded the old contraption and built an improved model that reset itself after each mouse. It was his first automatic weapon.

By 1861, Maxim had moved to another part of Maine and was operating a lathe—a type of wood-working machine—for a carpenter. He was there when the Civil War broke out in April. While Maxim avoided any involvement in the conflict, it nonetheless altered the rest of his life. Within

Richard Gatling (1818-1903) invented farming tools and studied medicine before creating what was then the world's most lethal weapon.

Of the approximately 615,000 soldiers to die in the Civil War, 204,000 were killed in battle. The other 411,000 perished from various infectious diseases.

months, Richard Jordan Gatling of Indianapolis, Indiana, would take a step that would lead directly to Hiram Maxim's destiny as the inventor of the automatic machine gun 23 years later.

In the summer of 1861, Gatling began work on a firearm that he hoped would, "by its rapidity of fire, enable one man to do as much battle duty as a hundred." He had decided to design the gun after witnessing battlefield conditions. The soldiers, he noticed, fell victim to disease more often than to enemy weapons. Since soldiers would always battle illness if they were forced to live together in large armies, Gatling's unusual solution was to do away with the need for large armies.

The mounted, hand-cranked gun Gatling eventually patented on November 4, 1862, was the first practical machine gun. Other inventors had tried to improve on the revolving-cylinder firearms made by Samuel Colt, then the quickest guns available. But only one innovator before Gatling had succeeded. In the closing months of 1861, Wilson Ager was selling the Union army his own mounted, hand-cranked machine gun. In Ager's single-barreled weapon, ammunition fed downward from a top-mounted hopper into the firing mechanism. To President Abraham Lincoln, the whole apparatus looked a lot like a giant coffee grinder. From then on, it was called the "coffee-mill gun."

But Ager's gun had severe limitations, chief among them its ammunition. Prepackaged metal cartridges that contained percussion cap, powder, and round all in one container—like the bullets we know today—were just then being introduced. The coffee-mill gun relied not on the new-style ammunition, but on metal tubes that had to be hand-filled by the operator with paper cartridges containing the gunpowder and lead bullets. A percussion cap then had to be fitted to the end of the tube. Just preparing the ammunition to load the weapon was very time consuming.

Although Gatling's first gun relied on hand-loaded tubes as well, he quickly redesigned it to fire the new cartridges. The new Gatling was much easier to load than Ager's weapon. Another advantage of the Gatling was its six-barreled design. Even today's barrels get extremely hot if a gun is fired continuously. The single-barreled coffee-mill gun was no exception. Gatling's multi-barreled design, on the other hand, spread the heat over six barrels. As a result, it could fire more rounds over a longer period of time than Ager's weapon.

Gatling's first models fired at the rate of 200 rounds per minute, a big improvement over the 120-round-per-minute limit of the coffee-mill gun. By 1876, the Gatling gun could fire 1,000 rounds per minute. Gatling continued to refine his weapon until by 1884 it could achieve an astounding rate of fire of 1,200 rounds per minute—20 bullets firing every second! Still, the Gatling gun wasn't capable of continuous firing while the trigger was pulled. Instead, a hand crank operated its firing mechanism. And that wasn't the weapon's only drawback; even the lightest Gatlings weighed over 90 pounds—too heavy for a single person to move.

Although the speed of firing was astounding on these hand-cranked guns, automatic machine guns are much more efficient—and horrifying—because they fire continuously for as long as the trigger is pulled.

Although they were initially thrilled with their manual machine guns, armies throughout the world eventually demanded a more useful weapon—one that was lighter than the Gatling, yet powerful enough to mow down entire columns of enemy soldiers with just the touch of a finger. But who could they turn to for such a perfect killing machine? This was most definitely a job for "a different breed" of mechanic.

That Hiram Maxim was capable of such an innovation, there was no doubt. After building his automatic mousetrap while still in his teens—an idea that someone else eventually patented—Maxim had gone on to more complex inventions. An automatic sprinkler system he created was the first of its kind to be activated by the fire itself. It soaked only the area burning and even transmitted an alarm through a telegraph line to the fire station.

Maxim's most important innovations before his work on the machine gun, however, were in lighting. He worked for several years on gas lighting, developing a system to regulate the flame. And he was at the forefront of the new field of electric lighting. His carbon-based electric lights were the first used in New York City, *before* the incandescent bulbs invented by Thomas Edison.

This work made Hiram Maxim a wealthy man. In 1881, he traveled to Europe to study the newest devices at the Electrical Exhibition in Paris. He wrote detailed descriptions of the lights, and then he visited the patent offices in France and Belgium to learn about all the electric lights that had been patented. But while Maxim was exhaustively examining electrical devices, Edison was cornering the market in the United States for his incandescent bulb. Perhaps that is why Maxim was willing to explore new avenues for his engineering talents.

A friend advised Maxim to forget all other inventions. "If you want to make a pile of money," he insisted, "invent something that will enable these Europeans to cut each other's throats with greater facility." The two were in Austria on business and had been talking about advances in electricity, but somehow the conversation had once again drifted to weaponry.

Thomas Edison (1847-1931) in 1881, the year he began promoting his electric lighting system in earnest

There was good reason for that. The year was 1882, and new threats of war were circulating through the capitals of Europe. Germany had gone to war three times in the last 18 years—against Denmark in 1864, Austria in 1866, and then France in 1870. Fighting had broken out in Bosnia and Herzegovina in 1875 and threatened to spread. Two years later, Russia and Romania had attacked Turkey. In short, when Maxim's friend suggested that a handsome profit awaited the inventor of a deadlier weapon, he was absolutely right.

Maxim finally succumbed to his friend's advice to improve upon the manual machine guns used by Europe's armies. In the end, the lure of riches didn't motivate him. Rather, it was that same old challenge of building and refining a machine that had always driven Maxim. Now, if he could only find a better way than a hand crank to drive a machine gun.

THE BREAKTHROUGH

For two years Maxim built and tested the different parts of a machine gun, trying to find a way to use the weapon's recoil. It was slow going since he had no previous model to follow. When he needed special tools, he made those, too. At last Maxim was ready to test the firing mechanism with live ammunition. The various components worked perfectly together, and the six test bullets were discharged in a lightning-quick, half-second burst. By the spring of 1884, Maxim had completed a working model of the entire gun.

Maxim's automatic machine gun worked exactly as he had expected. As long as he held the trigger, the gun's internal mechanism of springs and

An 1888 Maxim gun

levers captured the recoil energy and continued to fire all the ammunition. Maxim also devised a better way to feed bullets into the weapon. Earlier machine guns like Gatling's relied on some type of container mounted atop the weapon. The bullets then fell into the gun by force of gravity. While effective, such a system was impractical if a great many rounds were fired at once. To solve this problem, Maxim introduced a cloth belt that held the bullets side by side. Once the first round was loaded, the gun's recoil force sucked the belt in.

When tested, Maxim's finished model, introduced in 1885, spit out an astonishing 650 rounds per minute with almost no effort by the gunner. At 60 pounds, it was far lighter than the Gatling, which made it easier to transport in battle. It could also be taken apart easily for cleaning and minor repairs. And with the addition of a water-filled "jacket" wrapped around the barrel, the Maxim gun avoided the overheating problem that had plagued previous single-barreled machine guns.

Although the Gatling gun could fire more rounds per minute than the Maxim, cranking the Gatling was hard work. Another drawback was that soldiers had to be sitting or standing to fire the Gatling. Because a soldier could fire the Maxim while lying down, he was much better protected on the battlefield.

In the words of one historian, Maxim's weapon "swept the world as no other gun has done before or since." Its success was helped by the innovator himself, who toured Europe demonstrating his deadly machine. Austrian officers were awestruck that a weapon Maxim carried with just one arm and operated alone could produce such an impenetrable hail of lead. Maxim asked the Austrian commander in chief whether the gun fired fast enough. "Indeed," the amazed commander responded, "too fast. It is the most dreadful instrument that I have ever seen."

THE RESULT

By 1890, Maxim was supplying guns to Britain, Germany, Austria, Italy, Switzerland, and Russia. The king of Denmark, protesting that the weapon "would bankrupt the nation in ten minutes" because of the expense of the rounds of ammunition, wanted nothing to do with the gun. He was the exception.

Maxim's success led other innovators to consider alternate machine-gun designs. Since Maxim owned patents on all recoil systems, their only choice was to find other ways to power the gun. In 1889, John Moses Browning of the United States invented a machine gun that used gas from the exploding cartridge to operate the firing mechanism. Four years later an Austrian army captain by the name of Odkolek invented a better gas-operated machine gun. Odkolek immediately sold his idea to the Hotchkiss company in France and disappeared from history. The gun did not. Henceforth known as the Hotchkiss machine gun, it became famous.

In 1888, Archduke Franz Salvator (the Austrian emperor's son-in-law) and Count Dormus designed a small, lightweight machine gun that used a simple system of operation called "blowback." Remember, in recoil-operated guns, the weapon's kick operates the firing cycle. In machine guns driven by gas, a tube attached near the open end of the barrel captures gas from the fired round and routes it back to the breech area where it then operates the firing cycle. In a blowback gun, gas pressure from the escaping bullet literally blows the firing mechanism

back against a spring, which in turn pushes the mechanism forward to start the whole cycle again.

The first major battle between forces armed with the new automatic weapons took place during the Russo-Japanese War (1904-1905). The damage was so great that many military officers around the world accelerated their search for a way to protect soldiers from the dreadful effects of automatic fire.

By the beginning of World War I in 1914, most of the world's major armies had adopted the Maxim machine gun. Two countries on opposite sides in the war, Russia and Germany, each possessed 16,000 of the weapons by 1916, far more than any of the other combatants. The carnage reaped by the Maxims, especially the German guns trained against France and England on the western front, convinced British general Ernest Swinton of the need for

Maxim guns installed on U.S. Navy ships saw action in the Spanish-American War. This gunner on the USS Vixen fired his Maxim during the Battle of Santiago on July 3, 1898.

Most of the Allied forces had not yet made the machine gun central to their arsenals during World War I. This American gun crew fires 37 mm single-shot cannons at German machine gunners in the Argonne region of France in 1918.

armored battle vehicles. His brainchild was the tank, which thundered into action in September 1916.

Two months after the tank's debut, Hiram Maxim was dead at the age of 76. The automatic machine gun he invented continued to evolve quickly. General John T. Thompson of the United States Army developed a fire-from-the-hip blow-back gun at the end of World War I to "sweep" enemy trenches. When the war ended, so did the need for Thompson's "Trench Broom," as he called his weapon. Deciding to market the gun to civilian police, Thompson added "sub" to "machine gun" so the weapon wouldn't sound so warlike. The Thompson submachine gun—popularly known as the "Tommy gun"—was a huge hit, with gangsters as well as with police.

Today, automatic weapons come in all shapes and sizes, from pistols and assault rifles to vehicle- and aircraft-mounted machine guns. Perhaps the most frightening machine guns ever invented were electrically powered, multi-barreled Gatling guns, introduced in the 1960s and 1970s, which shot up to 10,000 rounds per minute. But since they were electrically powered, these monstrous guns were not automatic. Nor did they replace automatic machine guns, which today fire 600 to 800 rounds per minute, barely more than the 650-round-per-minute rate of the Maxim. Although gas-operated and blowback systems are now more often used, it wouldn't surprise Maxim that recoil remains a popular way to operate an automatic weapon. He had shown that he was a different—and better—breed of mechanic.

Caliber is the diameter of a bullet measured in millimeters or hundredths of inches. The M-2 machine gun, for example, fires bullets with a caliber of 13 millimeters (mm) or .50 inches.

Marines stationed in Saudi Arabia for Operation Desert Shield in 1991 pose with their automatic weapons, including a recoil-operated M-2 (on top of vehicle on the right), two gas-operated M-249s (on top of vehicle at left and held by the marine at far right), and gas-operated M-16 rifles (held by the three other standing marines).

CHAPTER SIX

Ernest Swinton
and the Tank

Throughout the history of land warfare, generals have strived to balance offensive power, protection of troops, and mobility. Chariots, first used as fighting vehicles in the sixth century B.C. by King Cyrus of Persia, are a good example. They sliced through enemy defenses aided by razor-sharp blades attached to their axles and undersides. Some chariots were fitted with wooden turrets, from which armored crews of four or more soldiers would throw javelins or shoot flaming arrows. When a greater punch was needed, Cyrus employed even bigger chariots filled with 20 soldiers and drawn into battle by teams of oxen. The use of chariots could backfire, though. The wheels could get stuck in mud or rough terrain, and a few well-aimed arrows could kill a chariot's horses or oxen. With the vehicle immobilized, the crew was doomed.

First used in Southeast Asia and parts of Africa, war elephants were another attempt to provide the

Major-General Ernest Swinton (1868-1951) lived and breathed the military as a soldier, officer, war correspondent, weapons inventor, and military historian.

Armies in India began using elephants in battle because horses were scarce, but leaders like Alexander the Great began using them, too, after facing the huge beasts in battle.

"big three" of striking power, mobility, and armor. Their use spread to other regions when Alexander the Great adopted elephants into the Greek army after battling the beasts during an invasion of India in 327 B.C. Crews of up to four soldiers rode the lumbering beasts into battle, hurling javelins from turrets atop the animals' backs. But elephants, like chariots, had their drawbacks. Chief among them was their nasty habit of turning around and trampling their own troops. The driver then had little choice but to hammer a metal spike into the rampaging animal's brain.

In addition to chariots and elephants, both Cyrus and Alexander used heavily armored horse soldiers. The cavalry galloped into battle wearing armored breastplates and helmets, carrying shields in one hand and 10-foot-long lances in the other. For those rare times when the troopers' lances failed them, they reached for the trusty swords stuffed in their belts. Because horse soldiers combined fire-power, mobility, and a fair amount of protection, they came to dominate most battlefields.

That began to change in the thirteenth century. New infantry weapons like pikes—lances up to 16 feet long—crossbows, and longbows spurred cavalry to adopt full suits of armor for themselves and their horses. But the extra 140 to 150 pounds severely reduced mobility. And when firearms were refined after the fourteenth century, even heavy armor was no protection. One new mobile defense was a high-walled wagon—an early tank.

This sixteenth-century tank was like a moving fortress that protected soldiers firing their guns.

With each century, a gunner's ability to kill the enemy improved. Matchlocks gave way to flintlocks, which moved aside for more reliable multi-shot weapons like Samuel Colt's revolvers and then Richard Gatling's hand-cranked machine gun. When armies demanded even deadlier weapons, Hiram Maxim supplied the first machine gun capable of loading and firing itself. During the first few months of World War I, Maxim's automatic weapon kept nearly all soldiers huddled in trenches—unable to move, let alone fight.

It was time for a weapon that allowed troops to move with protection, just as John Ericsson's *Monitor* had sheltered the sailor a half century earlier. One individual was considering just such a "land iron-clad" as he surveyed the battlefields of France in late 1914—Ernest Swinton of the British army.

Kaiser Wilhelm II (1859-1941) dreamed of creating a mighty German empire.

Ernest Swinton was born on October 21, 1868, to British parents in Bangalore, a large city in south-central India. His father was a judge in the British civil service in India, but the elder Swinton retired in August 1874, and the family moved to England. As an adult, Ernest Swinton became a military officer and a writer, twin passions that gave him the desire to improve the British armed forces and the creativity to figure out how to do it.

Shortly after becoming an engineering officer, Swinton was ordered to South Africa to battle the Boers, the region's inhabitants of Dutch descent. The Boer War (1899-1902) opened Swinton's eyes to the destructiveness of Britain's Maxim machine guns.

Automatic weapons played an even bigger role in the Russo-Japanese War (1904-1905) a few years later. Swinton wrote an official history of that war for the British government. As he reviewed the carnage, his dread of automatic fire grew.

When Germany's Kaiser Wilhelm II invaded Belgium and France in August 1914, the whole of Europe faced the horrors unleashed by Maxim's invention. The Germans advanced westward to a point about 30 miles from Paris, France. Their progress was finally checked in early September during the massive four-day Battle of the Marne, a struggle that pitted 1,275,000 Germans against 1,000,000 French and 125,000 British troops.

Everywhere during the battle automatic weapons cut swaths through formations of soldiers. In one all-night action, French machine gunners fired down a trench filled with German troops. The huddled Germans tried several times to surrender during the six hours of unrelenting fire. When the French gunners finally ceased, only 93 of the 550 Germans who had dug the trench the day before were able to climb out.

Soon after that battle, Swinton visited the front as an official war correspondent. He arrived just in time to witness a British and French counteroffensive that drove the Germans back, only to be ground to a bloody halt by German Maxims. Both sides dug networks of trenches to avoid the kill zone above ground. It was the beginning of the trench warfare that came to characterize World War I.

Swinton began wondering if an armored vehicle could defeat German machine guns. Armored cannon cars and machine-gun cars were being used by the British to support infantry assaults. As Swinton thought about transforming these vehicles, he might have recalled a science-fiction piece written by H. G. Wells in 1903. In that futuristic war story, the author imagined steam-powered "land ironclads" with skins of steel and 10-foot wheels.

While the idea of a wheeled ironclad had potential, this type of vehicle would have at least four major drawbacks—its wheels. They would never be able to cross artillery craters and trenches, break through barbed wire, or climb earthen defensive works. But what else could be used? Then, "like a beam from a lighthouse," the answer flashed across his mind. Just a few months earlier, he had been reading about the very contraption that was the answer to defeating the Germans.

Barbed wire, originally invented in the 1870s to fence ranches, was quickly adopted for military use. Enemies trying to cross through barbed-wire obstacles get stuck on the barbs, leaving them vulnerable to attack. The simple technology is still used today.

THE BREAKTHROUGH

The key was in a letter Swinton received in July 1914 from a mining engineer he had met in South Africa. The engineer mentioned an unusual farm machine being used in local mines. It could cross rough terrain, even trenches and holes, and easily pull a heavy plow through muddy ground. It could do all these things because it rode on "caterpillar" tracks instead of plain wheels.

Introduced in 1801 by an inventor named Thomas German, caterpillar tracks were continuous iron belts wrapped around a vehicle's wheels, one belt per side. German had discovered that the tracks spread a wagon's weight over a greater area than just the few points where normal wheels met the ground. As a result, the vehicle was less likely to get bogged down in muddy ground or sink in holes and trenches. Instead, it would just crawl steadily along like a caterpillar.

Swinton immediately saw the potential of an armored caterpillar tractor fitted with machine guns or cannons. Unfortunately, when Swinton broached the subject to military officials, few of them shared his confidence. Horatio Herbert Kitchener, the former commander of British forces during the Boer War and the current minister of war, flatly rejected the notion that a fleet of tractors could make any more headway against German barbed wire and machine guns than traditional infantry assaults.

The civilian head of the navy took a more progressive view. Under Winston Churchill, the navy was already building armored cars with naval-style revolving turrets. But the wheeled vehicles were unable to negotiate craters and trenches. In a letter to Herbert Henry Asquith, the prime minister, Churchill praised Swinton's idea of fitting caterpillar tractors with small bulletproof turrets. Such vehicles could crash through wire entanglements with their machine guns firing—an updated version of the chariots and heavy cavalry of old.

In 1909, five years before World War I began, Winston Churchill (right), then a member of Parliament, toured the German army ranks with Kaiser Wilhelm II. Wilhelm was the grandson of the long-reigning British queen Victoria, who had died in 1901.

Churchill's backing carried weight, and Kitchener eventually gave Swinton's tracked vehicle a chance. In a trial run on February 17, 1915, a caterpillar tractor hauling a 5,000-pound trailer (the approximate weight of armor and ammunition) got stuck in a flooded ditch. On the basis of that one test, the army ditched the idea of an armored tractor.

Once again it was Churchill who rescued Swinton's plan, offering navy money to fund development of the vehicle. There was a catch, however. Churchill had since shifted his focus. Instead of a tracked vehicle sporting a few machine guns, now he wanted a monster car 100 feet long and over 40 feet high, with six cannons housed in three turrets, all riding atop wheels measuring 40 feet in diameter. The problem was, while Churchill dreamed of a "land battleship," Swinton envisioned a smaller, more agile "machine-gun destroyer."

Churchill's concept was quickly shot down by the head of British artillery, who pointed out to the navy chief that German gunners couldn't help but hit such a huge target. Other ideas for vehicles followed, as various studies and tests tried to determine the most practical and effective shape that Swinton's conception should take. By summer 1915, Swinton was calling for several basic characteristics in the new vehicles: caterpillar tracks that would enable them to cross a trench at least eight feet wide, a top speed of four miles per hour so they would not outpace their supporting foot soldiers, and a revolving turret armed with either two Maxim machine guns or two cannons.

When the prototype, called "Little Willie," was finally completed in September, it was anything but little. The beast stood 7 feet, 8 inches high and 26 feet long, and its body and turret had room for eight crew members. There was only one problem—it didn't work very well. Because of its turret, Little Willie was top-heavy and unstable. Down below it was no better; its caterpillar tracks kept popping off the wheels. To solve the problem, the turret was discarded and the tracks were redesigned.

Finally, by the end of January 1916, "Big Willie" was finished. It was five feet longer and four

Little Willie after its turret was removed and tracks improved. By the time these alterations were made, however, both Swinton and the British army were more interested in a larger model of the tank.

Big Willie was also called "Mother" because it was the mother of the what was officially termed the Mark I tank corps. Ironically, Mother was a "male" tank packing powerful six-pound cannons. Male tanks were protected by one or two "female" tanks that had quick-firing machine guns.

inches higher than its little brother, and it came in two models, "male" and "female." The female was armed with six machine guns and the male with a combination of two cannons and four machine guns. Instead of a turret, Big Willie housed its weapons in side-mounted boxes called "sponsons."

By the first week in February, Big Willie had successfully completed its trials. The only thing left to do was to give the machine a real name. Hoping to confuse enemy spies on the lookout for any new weapons, Swinton rejected obvious names like "land-ship" or "land cruiser." Instead, he chose a word that described the unusual appearance of his creation but did not sound warlike. He decided to call it a "tank."

THE RESULT

The veil of secrecy was lifted when Big Willie rolled into battle for the first time on September 15, 1916, as part of the Somme offensive. Swinton had hoped the British would use a huge number of tanks to spearhead a single, war-ending attack. The British high command chose otherwise. Desperate to break the stalemate, the commanding general used the first tanks as soon as he got them. As a result, only 32 were available for the battle, sprinkled along a five-mile front in the midst of the advancing foot soldiers.

The tanks' performance was mixed. When they attacked in clusters (which, like the heavy cavalry of old, multiplied their "shock effect") the tanks gained ground. Groups of tanks had fewer problems overcoming barbed-wire entanglements, trenches, artillery craters, and machine-gun nests than lone tanks. Vehicles forced to attack by themselves, as most did, became easy targets for every enemy weapon within range. Often, the tanks were disabled before they could do any damage.

Another problem during the Somme offensive was the metal-piercing bullet just introduced by the Germans to battle other armored vehicles. Maxim rounds that should have bounced off the tanks penetrated the armor and hit the horrified men within.

Despite the shortcomings, German reaction to the assault was proof the new weapons had gotten the enemy's attention. After the battle, German commanders in the field reported that "the enemy in the latest fighting have employed new engines of

A Mark I lumbers over the top of a trench. It was clear to the British, who had suffered tremendous losses from German machine-gun fire, that the tanks saved lives.

war, as cruel as [they are] effective." Everywhere tanks were used, German surrenders increased.

In subsequent battles, tanks were given the chance to fight as their creator originally had envisioned. On November 17, 1917, the first day of the Battle of Cambrai, 324 of the armored behemoths led the attack along a six-mile front. That's an average of one tank every 97 feet, which was much better than the September ratio of one tank every 825 feet. "The triple belts of [barbed] wire were crossed as if they had been beds of nettles," reported one British participant, "and 350 pathways were sheared through them for the infantry." The soldier was wrong about the number of tanks, but he was absolutely right about the "grotesque and terrifying" appearance of the tanks. At the end of the first day, the British offensive had broken five miles into the enemy's rear flank and taken 4,000 German prisoners.

Unfortunately, many of the tanks experienced mechanical failure, and German artillery destroyed others. The tanks were especially vulnerable in the narrow streets of towns because buildings blocked their maneuvering. Quick-thinking enemy soldiers took advantage of the clumsy beasts by tying several grenades together and throwing them under the tanks. The explosion usually blew their tracks off. On November 27, the British offensive ground to a halt due to winter weather.

Despite the drive's ultimate failure, the tanks' ability to combine armor, firepower, and mobility had been clearly proven. Had additional infantry troops been available to exploit the gaps initially made by the tanks, the British might have celebrated an overwhelming victory instead of another frustrating draw. As it was, the territory the tanks helped the British gain in the first few hours at Cambrai was comparable to the gains they had made in three months during the earlier Third Battle of Ypres.

Cambrai convinced all sides to produce tanks as quickly as possible. The Germans launched their own landship, called the A7V, while the French introduced the Renault tank. Other models from Russia and the United States followed. The era of armored warfare had begun.

Lasting from July to October 1917, the Third Battle of Ypres was the deadliest of four bloody battles near Ypres, Belgium. The British suffered over 244,000 casualties to gain just four miles of enemy territory.

"We were not beaten by the genius of Marshal Foch [commander of the Allied forces], but by "General Tank."
—General A. D. H. von Zwehl, German military historian

The highly decorated Major-General Ernest Swinton himself retired from warfare. As an official war correspondent, he was writing about the war even as it unfolded, and he later wrote a book called *Eyewitness* about his development of the tank. Swinton taught military history at Oxford University from 1925 to 1939 and was knighted for his accomplishments. Appointed commander of the Royal Tank Corps in 1934, he oversaw the military use of his creation. The inventor died in 1951.

Over the years, tanks and their ability to kill have evolved dramatically. They've gotten bigger, for one thing. Big Willie weighed 28 tons, and heavy tanks in the 1930s weighed as much as 40 tons, but the tracks of the American M1A2 Abrams carry almost 60 tons today.

And tanks have gotten faster. The Abrams— the world's premier battletank—can travel at over 40 miles per hour, about as fast as a World War II tank and 10 times faster than the walking speed of Big Willie.

Of course, the present-day tank's destructive ability is far beyond anything Swinton or Churchill could have imagined. The Abrams, for example, fires a 120 mm fin-stabilized round—a shell over 4.7 inches in diameter that uses tiny fins for stabilization. One popular type of shell used by the Abrams is the High-Explosive Anti-Tank (HEAT) round, which is designed to explode just short of an enemy tank. The force from the blast rips a hole in the foe's armor, through which the hot metal shards of the exploded round travel. The enemy tank is burned to a crisp from the inside. Laser range-finders and thermal-imaging sights that illuminate the enemy even in dense smoke or complete darkness ensure that the Abrams rarely misses its mark.

Many of today's armored vehicles can even travel on water. The American-designed M113 armored personnel carrier floats like a boat; crews of other tanks can erect canvas water-barriers around the outer edges to improve flotation. The M2 and M3 Bradley fighting vehicles of the United States use this method to "swim."

With all that the descendants of Swinton's brainchild can do today, there's one thing that no modern battletank has yet to do—turn and stampede its own troops. That's a good thing, because few soldiers today carry hammers and metal stakes!

Soldiers drive an M3 Bradley in Saudi Arabia during Operation Desert Shield, the defensive military operation before the drive into Iraq that ended the Persian Gulf War.

CHAPTER SEVEN

Walter Dornberger and Wernher von Braun and the Ballistic Missile

Five years after the beginning of World War II, Londoners first experienced the weapon that Nazi dictator Adolf Hitler hoped would snatch victory from the grasp of England and the other Allies. On September 8, 1944, the world's first rocket-propelled ballistic missile exploded in a suburb of London, killing 2 people, injuring 20 others, and destroying 38 homes. The day before, the missile had been known as the A-4. Thereafter, the Nazis called it Vergeltungswaffe 2—German for "weapon of retaliation number two"—or simply, the V-2.

Several scientists helped develop the V-2, the most famous of whom was Wernher von Braun. Von Braun's dream had been to construct a rocket for space travel, not to build a weapon. It was Walter Dornberger, an artillery officer in the German army, who harnessed von Braun's knowledge of rocketry to create the weapon we know as the V-2, the forerunner of all present-day ballistic missiles.

A ballistic missile is powered by a rocket engine for the first part of its flight. When its fuel runs out at the highest point along the flight trajectory, it continues along its trajectory (like a thrown ball) until it hits its target.

Walter Dornberger (1895-1980), at left in hat, and Wernher von Braun (1912-1977), with arm in cast, when they were captured by Allied forces just before Germany's surrender in 1945. Another staff member, Herbert Axster, stands between them. Top military engineers for the Germans in World War II, both Dornberger and von Braun moved to the United States and continued to be leaders in the field of rocketry.

105

German dictator Adolf Hitler (1889-1945), at left, with leader of the German air force Hermann Göring (1893-1946), waving to a crowd of supporters. Hitler was slow to see that the rocket could be a useful weapon, but Göring was immediately fascinated with the possibilities.

The story of the V-2 began in 1929, the end of the turbulent decade following World War I. On the heels of defeat in the First World War, Germany was forced to demilitarize. The victorious nations slashed the German army from 9 million soldiers to 100,000, and Germany was prohibited from building an air force. More importantly, the Germans were forbidden to stock any artillery with a range beyond 17 miles. With no air force and no long-range artillery, Germany possessed no way to strike deep behind enemy lines in case of another war.

There was a loophole in the war-ending 1918 Treaty of Versailles, however. Because the science of rocketry was still in its infancy, the victors never thought to prohibit ballistic missiles. A decade later, Germany used this oversight to develop the V-2.

In 1929, a captain named Karl Becker was working in the German army's weapons department. After watching a movie about a fictional trip to the moon, Becker was struck by the possibility of using rockets as substitutes for artillery. He issued a report to the defense ministry about the potential of rocket-propelled weapons and was granted permission to undertake research. In 1930, Becker ordered his new assistant, artillery captain Walter Dornberger, to develop a rocket with greater range and destructive capability than any previous artillery cannon.

Born in August 1895, Dornberger as a boy had cherished hopes of becoming an architect. But his father, a pharmacist, insisted that Walter join the army. In Germany before the First World War, being an army officer was a great honor that would give Walter entrance into the highest level of society. Within months of his enlistment in August 1914, Dornberger was promoted to the rank of second lieutenant in an artillery unit. In the terrible combat conditions of the western front during World War I, he became an expert in using artillery.

Shortly before the war ended in November 1918, Dornberger was captured and sent to a French prisoner-of-war camp, where he spent the next two years. After his release, he served another four years on active duty in Germany. Then he took time off to earn a degree in mechanical engineering at the Berlin Technical University. He had just graduated

When the first liquid-fuel rocket was launched by American Robert Goddard in 1926, there were a number of German scientists also working on rocketry. The Germans did not learn of Goddard's achievement for another decade, and even then reports were vague. The work of Dornberger and von Braun was not influenced by Goddard's rocket.

It is scientifically impossible to shoot artillery much farther than the Paris gun's 80-mile range. Why? Gas pressure from the explosion of the main charge in a gun powers the shell, and the amount of time the gas can act on the shell determines how far and fast the shell can travel. To outshoot the Paris gun would require a barrel length of about 1.2 miles.

A rocket is not like the bullet of a gun, but rather like the entire gun. When a gun is fired, expanding gases within the barrel discharge the bullet. The action causes a reaction—the recoil of the weapon against the firer's shoulder. When a rocket's fuel is ignited, the explosive gases spit out the back, just like a bullet leaving a gun. The rocket moves forward in a reaction like a gun's recoil. This all happens because of Newton's Third Law of Motion: For every action there is an equal and opposite reaction.

in the spring of 1930 when Becker tapped him for the rocket assignment.

Dornberger knew a lot about the gun Becker had just ordered him to surpass—Germany's massive Paris gun of World War I. Each of the seven huge Paris guns had a 117-foot-long barrel that was capable of launching 25-pound explosive shells from German territory all the way to the streets of Paris, France—a distance of 80 miles. Dornberger knew it was impractical to build a barrel long or strong enough to fire any farther, so he agreed with Becker that rockets were the only option if Germany were ever again to command a long-range military threat. Unfortunately, the artillery captain knew almost nothing about rocketry.

The weapons department offered little help. In 1930, it ran a small testing facility where Captain Becker was developing simple gunpowder rockets designed to fire in large groups at targets three to five miles away. Dornberger realized that if he was going to outshoot the Paris gun, he would have to start with Becker's batch of simple missiles. These weapons hadn't really changed since their introduction in the first decade of the 1800s by England's William Congreve, who had been, like Dornberger, an artillery officer.

Congreve's rockets were the culmination of centuries of development. In fact, gunpowder missiles were nearly as old as gunpowder itself. "Fire arrows"—gunpowder rockets capable of flying as far as 1,000 feet—were developed by the Chinese sometime between the tenth and twelfth centuries.

English monk Roger Bacon is believed to have been the first person in Europe to learn of gunpowder, probably from some unrecorded traveler to the Far East. In the 1240s, Bacon buried the ingredients to gunpowder in a strange word puzzle for fear of being accused by church leaders of dealing with magic. If the right amounts of saltpeter, sulfur, and charcoal were combined, wrote Bacon, the "light of lightning and the sound of thunder can be perfectly imitated." Bacon then described launching the mixture "over long distances" to "destroy a town or an army." It's possible he was talking about rockets. Less than a century later, when people discovered that the powder could launch a stone from the open end of a tube, the gun was born and Bacon's mysterious mixture acquired the name gunpowder.

Roger Bacon (c.1220-1292) examines a book on alchemy, the chemistry of his time.

Gunpowder rockets were adopted by armies throughout Europe. The French used rockets to defend their forts and to attack those of the enemy, and Holland, Germany, Italy, and Greece experimented with military forms of fire-arrows. Of course, rockets also found use as plain old fireworks.

In 1804, after witnessing rocket attacks on British troops in India, Congreve began developing rocket-powered artillery weapons. His rockets, which weighed anywhere from 3 to 12 pounds, could take off from land or boats and fly as far as a mile and a half. They carried warheads filled with shrapnel or a flammable liquid that burned whatever it touched.

Over the next decade, the British made extensive use of Congreve's fire-arrows. During the War of 1812, British rockets bombarded Fort McHenry,

British army officer Henry Shrapnel put grapeshot—grape-sized iron balls—into an iron cannonball in 1804. When the cannonball exploded over enemy troops, the grapeshot rained down like dozens of bullets. In time, all fragments from exploding shells became known as **shrapnel**.

which guarded Baltimore, Maryland. During the night of September 13, 1814, a young American lawyer named Francis Scott Key witnessed the attack while supervising a prisoner exchange aboard a British ship anchored in Chesapeake Bay. When Key awoke the next morning "by dawn's early light," he saw the flag atop Fort McHenry still flying. "The rockets' red glare" had ceased by then, and the relieved American jotted down the words that eventually became America's national anthem.

In this romantic painting, Key gazes on his young nation's flag flying triumphant over Fort McHenry a few months before the end of the War of 1812.

More than a century later, gunpowder rockets had not advanced much, and Dornberger knew they would be useless for his purposes. Gunpowder rockets did not function reliably, and they could not be mass produced. Worst of all, they were far too limited in their range.

Dornberger had no choice but to develop from scratch a new kind of rocket that burned liquid fuel. What little was known about liquid-fuel engines suggested they operated predictably. And liquid fuel could be readily produced by Germany's advanced chemical industry. Most importantly, the range of liquid-fuel rockets was theoretically unlimited.

In 1932, it was Dornberger's good fortune to meet Wernher von Braun, a 20-year-old student of rocketry. Von Braun was born in March 1912 in Wirsitz, Germany, in the province of Posen (now part of Poland). The son of a provincial magistrate, Wernher went to the best private schools. He did poorly in mathematics at first, but one day the 12-year-old read a magazine article describing an imaginary trip to the moon. From that moment on, Wernher developed a passion for space flight, and his performance in math—the subject an aerospace engineer would need most—improved so much that one of his teachers told his parents, "Wernher is a genius. He will do great things."

In pursuit of his dream, von Braun was testing a liquid-fuel rocket in a Berlin field in the spring of 1932 when he was approached by Dornberger. The artillery officer had gone to the field, a favorite testing ground for amateur rocket enthusiasts, looking

Von Braun made his first rocket-propelled vehicle at age 12 by strapping six large skyrockets to his wagon. When the fireworks exploded, the wagon rocketed out of control with the delighted boy on board.

At the time, none of us thought of the havoc which rockets would eventually wreak as weapons of war.
—Wernher von Braun

for help. When Dornberger offered the young man a job as his chief assistant, von Braun eagerly accepted, even though he wanted to build a rocket to reach the moon, not a missile to attack another country.

The two quickly set to work hiring other scientists and technicians. "It was not easy at first to get my young collaborators away from their space dreams," Dornberger later wrote. The group's immediate goal was to successfully test a rocket engine fueled by liquid oxygen and gasoline. Everything had to be done from scratch since the field was so new.

When the time came to test the group's first rocket engine on December 21, 1932, von Braun and Dornberger felt immense pride in what they had accomplished in just a few months. Their rosy feelings didn't last, however. Within seconds after the start of the test, the experimental engine had disappeared in a cloud of dense, foul-smelling smoke. The motor had blown up as soon as von Braun, crouching 12 feet from the engine's test platform, ignited it with a long match.

Three weeks later, the second engine was ready for testing. After just a few seconds, it, too, was destroyed, this time from intense heat. Frustration mounted as the team continued to test various fuel mixtures, fuel-injection systems, and methods of cooling the engine during operation. Finally, after several months, Dornberger's team got an engine to run consistently over several tests. Now all they had to do was to design and build the rocket's body.

Dornberger already had a good idea of how a successful ballistic missile should perform. For every 1,000 feet of flight, he insisted the rocket strike no farther than 2 to 3 feet from the center of its target. No Congreve-type rocket or artillery round could do that. In addition, the missile had to be transportable over existing roads and railways. Dornberger made sure the transport vehicle could serve as the rocket launcher. With the final addition of a 2,200-pound explosive warhead, the V-2 missile that he eventually developed was history's most destructive weapon.

When planning the test version of the missile, Dornberger's team first considered the problem of stabilizing the weapon during flight. Since artillery shells fired from rifled bores achieve stability by spinning, Dornberger suggested they design the missile to spin on its axis like a huge bullet. The others quickly objected. Centrifugal force would plaster the spinning rocket's liquid fuel against the outer sides of the fuel tanks, causing the engine to sputter to a stop. The group finally decided instead to place gyroscopes inside the weapon's nose.

Designated the A-2, the test missile flew to an altitude of a mile and a half in December 1934. Over the next several years, Dornberger and von Braun continued to tinker with the A-2. What eventually emerged was a 21-foot-long, 1,650-pound missile they renamed the A-3. In December 1937, tests of the A-3 were conducted at Peenemünde, their new secret research station in north Germany on the Baltic Sea. The A-3 failed the trials, mainly because of its revamped guidance system. This problem took

First used in a torpedo by Robert Whitehead in 1895, gyroscopes also became the principal means to control the flight of the Germans' missile when it was built. The V-2's guidance system would use three gyroscopes to guide the missile through its flight.

the team another two years to solve. As one thing after another went wrong, the stakes grew higher, for the Germans were gearing up for war.

The site of Peenemünde was chosen for its isolation. There it was possible to hide the top-secret new weapon being developed. The scientists also needed money and skilled workers to run the massive facility, and it was a constant struggle for Dornberger to obtain from the German authorities what was required to build his rockets.

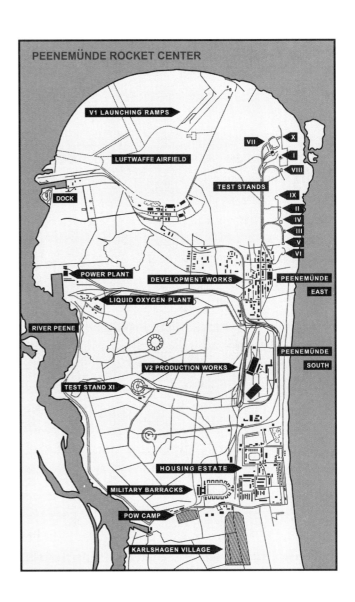

PEENEMÜNDE ROCKET CENTER

V1 LAUNCHING RAMPS

VII   X

LUFTWAFFE AIRFIELD   I

VIII

TEST STANDS

IX

DOCK   II

IV

III

V

VI

POWER PLANT   DEVELOPMENT WORKS   PEENEMÜNDE

EAST

LIQUID OXYGEN PLANT

RIVER PEENE

PEENEMÜNDE

SOUTH

V2 PRODUCTION WORKS

TEST STAND XI

HOUSING ESTATE

MILITARY BARRACKS

POW CAMP

KARLSHAGEN VILLAGE

THE BREAKTHROUGH

Using what they had learned from the less-than-stellar performance of the A-3, Dornberger and von Braun began developing the more advanced A-4. The first challenge was to build an improved engine. Through tests, the team had determined the missile would have to fly faster than 3,350 miles per hour (almost a mile per second), more than three times the speed of any previously manufactured craft. Such an engine would require a new type of fuel pump. The group was stymied until von Braun stumbled upon just the right pump in an unlikely spot—a factory that built water pumps for firefighting equipment.

The group was on the brink of success when Adolf Hitler started World War II. Hitler's Nazi Party had gained support from German voters in the early 1930s, and in January 1933 Hitler became chancellor. Within months, some of the twentieth century's most momentous events occurred. Hitler shelved the constitution, made himself dictator, and set Germany on a course for world conquest.

In 1938 Germany annexed first Austria and part of Czechoslovakia and then took the rest of Czechoslovakia early in 1939. Great Britain and France finally drew a line at the border of Poland. With Hitler's invasion of Poland on September 1, 1939, World War II began. As the Nazis earmarked funds to pay for the war, experimental programs like Dornberger's suffered. As a result, the A-4 wouldn't be ready for its first test flight until early 1942.

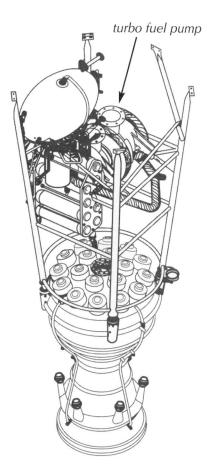

turbo fuel pump

The size of the A-4/V-2 rocket motor required a number of innovations, most notably the turbo fuel pump adopted from firefighting equipment.

The team's long wait did not end happily. As the first A-4 sat in its test stand during a pre-flight engine trial, it slipped free and was destroyed by the fall. Tests of the next two A-4s also failed. The first one lifted off well enough on June 13, 1942, only to roll over seconds into its flight and nosedive into the nearby Baltic Sea. Two months after that disaster, a third A-4 blasted off. Forty-five seconds into its flight, this rocket ended much like the others. Dornberger and von Braun could only sift through mounds of data and hope for one more shot.

They got it on October 3, 1942. Another failure, Dornberger knew, would likely mean an abrupt halt to their government funding and a waste of years of tedious work. "This was," he wrote, "the final verdict."

One of Dornberger's rockets being elevated to its vertical firing position

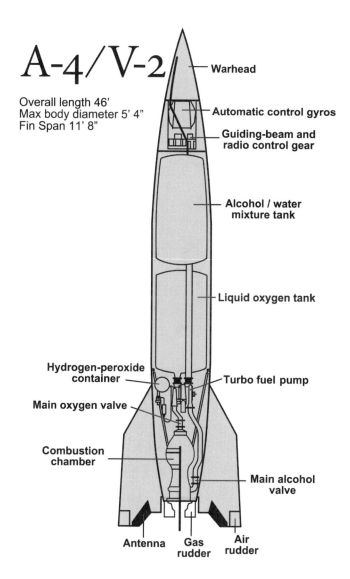

A-4/V-2

Overall length 46'
Max body diameter 5' 4"
Fin Span 11' 8"

- Warhead
- Automatic control gyros
- Guiding-beam and radio control gear
- Alcohol / water mixture tank
- Liquid oxygen tank
- Hydrogen-peroxide container
- Turbo fuel pump
- Main oxygen valve
- Combustion chamber
- Main alcohol valve
- Antenna
- Gas rudder
- Air rudder

A diagram of the A-4 rocket, showing the turbo fuel pump that provided the necessary power and the automatic gyroscopes that kept the rocket on course

In its last chance for success, the A-4 performed flawlessly. The 28,400-pound missile soared to a world record height of almost 53 miles—more than twice as high as a shell from the Paris gun.

One of Dornberger's historic rockets is launched. Dornberger wept with joy when his A-4 succeeded.

When it landed 120 miles away, the A-4 struck within two and a half miles of its target. While not exactly a bull's-eye, the team considered the flight a triumph because the rocket did not blow up early. The impact itself was spectacular, with the ballistic missile crashing into the calm waters of the Baltic Sea with a force of 50 speeding train engines.

The missile had not quite "invaded space," as Dornberger claimed at a celebration that evening. But its 53 miles of altitude only missed that goal by about 4 miles. Space flight was not the priority in any case. "So long as the war lasts," Dornberger remarked, "our most urgent task can only be the rapid perfecting of the rocket as a weapon." Space travel would have to wait for peacetime.

THE RESULT

After watching a newsreel of the successful October launch, Adolf Hitler declared the A-4 "the decisive weapon of the war" and authorized production of 2,000 ballistic missiles per month. A British raid on Dornberger's testing facility in August 1943, however, slowed production of the missiles.

On September 8, 1944, the rocket bombing of England began. Over the next six and a half months, the ballistic missile—renamed the V-2—killed approximately 2,500 Londoners. The Allies finally put an end to the "rain" of terror when they overran the missiles' launch facilities on March 29, 1945.

Bomb damage near St. Paul's Cathedral in central London. The Germans deliberately chose non-military targets for their "weapon of retaliation."

When the war ended, the German team was working on an intercontinental ballistic missile (ICBM). This two-stage missile would use one rocket to launch; then, high in the atmosphere, the first stage would drop off and a second rocket—and warhead—would fly all the way to the United States.

A Peacekeeper ICBM. ICBMs can be launched to hit targets virtually anywhere in the world.

Before the war in Europe ended in May, von Braun and Dornberger were captured by U.S. forces. After the war, von Braun willingly moved to the United States to work on America's infant rocket program. His contributions include overseeing the development of the Jupiter C booster rocket. The Jupiter launched the first U.S. satellite (*Explorer I*) into orbit in January 1958 and lifted the first American, astronaut Alan Shepard, into suborbital space in May 1961. And a team under von Braun developed the Saturn V rocket that took astronaut Neil Armstrong to the moon in July 1969. Wernher von Braun died on June 16, 1977.

Dornberger also immigrated to America after the war. Until 1950, he helped the U.S. Air Force develop air-launched missiles. From 1950 until his retirement in 1965, he worked as the chief scientist for the Bell Aerospace Corporation in Buffalo, New York. After retiring, Walter Dornberger returned to Germany, where he died in June 1980.

Before their deaths, Dornberger and von Braun witnessed the evolution of the weapon they helped to create. The variety of strategic ballistic missiles in existence today boggles the mind. The Russian-made SS-18, for example, can travel up to 7,450 miles with an armament of eight nuclear warheads. Each warhead can be programmed to hit its own target 20 or more miles away from the others. A single SS-18 can thus largely disable an enemy in one blow. The Minuteman III of the United States can carry three independently targeted nuclear warheads a total distance of 8,070 miles. Both nations

A Minuteman III missile in a storage silo about 60 miles from Grand Forks, North Dakota. The silo is also the missile's launcher, controlled by a separate launching facility. The United States has 1,000 silo-launched ICBMs.

also have shorter-range tactical nuclear ballistic missiles designed for use against large concentrations of troops and tanks or other battlefield targets.

William Congreve would gasp in awe at what his rockets have become. As Roger Bacon wrote of his mysterious powder, "much light can be created accompanied by a horrible fracas." The powder, he warned, could "destroy a town or an army." Bacon saw the horrific potential from the start.

Strategic missiles are long-range weapons that target cities, military installations, and the like to destroy an enemy's ability to make war. **Tactical missiles** are short-range weapons that destroy troops, tanks, ships, and other battlefield targets in order to defeat an enemy in a war.

Weapons of the Future

It stands to reason that as innovators create more advanced weapons, warfare will become increasingly destructive. Surprisingly, the opposite seems to be happening. Part of the reason lies in sophisticated technology. Smart bombs and new kinds of missiles, torpedoes, depth charges, and machine guns can destroy targets with little or no human input. That's not only safer for the military personnel using them, but also for those on the receiving end, especially civilians. You see, unlike bombs from decades past, smart weapons don't have to destroy whole cities, tens of thousands of civilians, or entire armies to eliminate an enemy's ability to make war. Got an enemy arms factory nestled between two apartment complexes? Then send in a few Tomahawk cruise missiles, like those made famous during the Persian Gulf War (1991). Launched from ships, subs, or planes as far away as 780 miles, the Tomahawks can level that arms factory in about 75 minutes—without touching the apartments. And they'll do it at night when the factory is empty.

A B-2 Stealth bomber eludes enemy radar with its special shape and radar-absorbing exterior. Its pricetag is about $2 billion. During the 1999 war in Yugoslavia, B-2s flew from their base in Missouri to fire satellite-guided bombs at enemy targets, at a cost of $1.6 million for a single bombing run.

The United States also dropped "soft bombs" on Yugoslavia in 1999. These bombs contain graphite filament and charged carbon particles that coat electrical wires to disrupt power. They cause no permanent damage.

GBU-24 precision-guided penetrators on an F-15 Eagle. "Smart bombs" such as these became household knowledge during the Persian Gulf War because they could be guided into spaces as narrow as a chimney.

This type of high-tech war was showcased in spring 1999 during the war between the American-led North Atlantic Treaty Organization (NATO) and Yugoslavia. Using about 1,000 state-of-the-art warplanes, NATO pounded Yugoslav targets for 78 days. While NATO did lose an F-117A Nighthawk (Stealth) fighter jet, not a single NATO soldier was killed or missing in combat. (Even the Nighthawk pilot was promptly rescued.) Civilians in Yugoslavia also suffered less than noncombatants in traditional wars. To be sure, some civilian industries, like automobile factories that could help the war effort, were intentionally hit. Still, considering that NATO bombers flew 35,000 missions that destroyed many military vehicles, much of Yugoslavia's military industry and electrical power plants, as well as scores of roads and bridges, the misery experienced by Yugoslav civilians was generally not excessive.

A big reason for less destruction is more accurate weapons. Laser-guided bombs from American

F-117s and satellite-guided bombs from U.S. B-2 Stealth bombers can be directed to strike only vital military targets. In World War II, a bomber had to level an entire city block to ensure destruction of a single building; four decades later during the Persian Gulf War, smart bombs from F-117s could obliterate a similar building by flying down its chimney! Although NATO bombs in Yugoslavia were not foolproof, smart bombs were used there in place of ground troops. Not only were the lives of NATO infantry soldiers spared by this decision, but also the lives of a great many Yugoslav troops.

The French-made Exocet sea-skimming missile is a good example of how some smart weapons work. Fired from air, sea, or land, sea skimmers initially rely on their launch vessel to paint an enemy ship with its radar. This information then guides the

An F-117 lands in Saudi Arabia during the Persian Gulf War's Operation Desert Storm. Like the B-2, the F-117 is a stealth bomber, invisible to enemy radar. The one that was shot down in Yugoslavia was probably detected by human eyes, not high-tech anti-aircraft equipment.

Radar, which stands for **ra**dio **d**etecting **a**nd **r**anging, determines the location of an object by measuring the length of time it takes radio waves to strike the object and be reflected back.

missile. As the launching vessel turns to another task, the sea skimmer continues to its target, updating the original radar image with information it gathers itself. The missile's impact drives its warhead deep into the target ship's hull, where the explosion rips the vessel apart.

Okay, this isn't exactly bloodless for the particular target's crew, but many ships today have more than a fighting chance thanks to their own smart defenses. The Vulcan-Phalanx, an electrically powered Gatling gun, performs like a whole battalion of machine gunners on alert. Mounted on a ship's deck, the Vulcan-Phalanx detects incoming missiles 5,600 yards away with its radar. When a missile is within 2,500 yards, the Vulcan-Phalanx lets loose a hail of bullets that destroys the incoming projectile.

A Vulcan-Phalanx close-in weapon system aboard the USS Nimitz

The downside to high-tech weapons is their great expense. Take the Tomahawk cruise missile. Each 2,650-pound Tomahawk costs about $1 million. How about those 20 mm shells fired from the Vulcan-Phalanx? Every round costs $20. That's $11,000 for a five-second shot burst—about what you might pay for a typical compact car. Like the Danish king who balked at the cost of feeding ammunition to Hiram Maxim's machine gun, most countries can't afford to even operate sophisticated weapons, let alone own them.

As a result, poorer nations will continue to rely on more traditional tanks, artillery, planes, and munitions. They have more frightening options, as well. Remember Caesar's catapults that launched dead bodies over the walls of enemy forts? That was an

early form of biological warfare. Generals no longer pitch corpses over walls, but they can fire just a few primitive missiles or artillery rounds loaded with bacteria or viruses and wipe out enemy cities or troop concentrations. Bacteria like anthrax or pneumonic plague can wipe out whole cities in as little as three to four days.

Chemical weapons are another inexpensive way to kill. Delivered mainly by artillery and aircraft, nerve agents like Sarin gas and VX liquid cause paralysis and eventually death. Other chemicals called herbicides, like the Agent Orange defoliant used by American forces in the Vietnam War, destroy enemy troops indirectly by killing the foliage that hides them and the crops that feed them.

But the weapon offering the most bang for the buck is the nuclear-explosive device. Compare these following examples. In a raid in February 1945,

A Tomahawk cruise missile fired at an Iraqi target during the Persian Gulf War. Satellite-guided Tomahawks were used against Yugoslavia in 1999. Unlike laser-guided bombs, these missiles use the global positioning system to guide the bombs in any weather condition.

The eight nations known to have nuclear weapons are the United States, Russia, France, China, the United Kingdom, Israel, India, and Pakistan.

hundreds of Allied bombers in three waves dropped over 650,000 incendiary bombs (non-nuclear explosives especially designed to cause fires) on the German city of Dresden. The firestorm that followed left 135,000 people dead. Six months later, a lone U.S. bomber dropped a crude atomic bomb over Hiroshima, Japan. Within minutes, 78,000 people had either disappeared in the explosion or lay dying from radiation poisoning.

Now, if poorer nations still have access to old-style arms and relatively inexpensive weapons of mass destruction, why is warfare still becoming less destructive? For one thing, warfare itself is tolerated less by world opinion than at any time in the past. This is true of high-tech weapons, too; but it is especially so for older and cheaper weapons that kill indiscriminately. In an age of global economies, it just doesn't pay to be seen by potential trading partners as a barbaric nation. Another reason is that clever innovators aren't just inventing new weapons; they are also devising ways to defeat weapons. For example, America's Strategic Defense Initiative (SDI, or Star Wars) recently completed its first successful test in June 1999. Simulating an incoming ballistic missile, a U.S. Army test rocket flying at supersonic speed was intercepted and obliterated by a 20-foot-long High-Altitude Area Defense missile. It now appears ballistic missiles might one day meet the same fate. We can only hope that humanity's awesome power to innovate will ultimately lead not just to violence and destruction, but also to better and better ways to prevent bloodshed.

GLOSSARY

aircraft carrier: a ship that is designed to serve as an airbase, with hangars and runways

armor: a covering, often metal, to protect the body or a ship or vehicle from attack

artillery: large-caliber weapons such as cannons or missile launchers

Asroc: **a**nti-**s**ubmarine **roc**ket; a rocket-propelled torpedo that is launched by a ship or airplane. Once over its submarine target, the torpedo separates and dives.

balance chamber: the part of a Whitehead torpedo in which a disk-shaped valve rigged to a system of levers keeps the weapon on course

ballast: a weight, such as rocks, sand, or water, which is put in a hold of a ship or submarine or the gondola of a hot-air balloon to enhance stability or control ascent and descent

ballistic: something that follows an arced path after being thrown (like a ball) or launched or shot (like a cannonball or bullet)

ballistic missile: a rocket that is allowed to fall freely, following a path like a thrown ball, after being launched and reaching a predetermined location under rocket power; *see also* **intercontinental ballistic missile**

barbed wire: a type of wire with sharply pointed barbs. Developed for ranching, it was quickly adopted for military use as an obstacle.

barrel: the metal tube of a firearm through which a bullet travels when it is fired

battleship: the largest type of warship, clad with thick armor and loaded with big cannons

biological warfare: warfare in which dangerous viruses or bacteria are released on enemy forces

blowback: a type of automatic machine gun that is powered by a combination of the gas pressure of bullets as they are fired and a spring within the breech

bore: the inside of the barrel of a gun

breech: the closed end of a gun's barrel

broadside ship: a large wooden sailing warship with lines of guns mounted on a gun deck; the warship used by the world's great navies from the 1500s to the 1800s

Browning gun: an automatic machine gun, invented by John Moses Browning, which is powered with the captured gas of the exploding cartridge

caliber: the diameter of the bore of a firearm or the diameter of a bullet or cannonball, measured in millimeters or hundredths of an inch

cannon: a large mounted weapon that shoots heavy projectiles

casualty: someone who is killed, wounded, captured, or missing in action in battle

catapult: a mechanical artillery device, using counterweights or twisted rope for power, which hurls objects, such as stones, at enemies

caterpillar tracks: continuous chain treads fitted over wheels on tractors or tanks to allow the vehicles to travel over muddy or broken terrain

cavalry: troops on horseback; now, highly mobile troops in vehicles

chariot: a two-wheeled vehicle drawn by a horse in ancient times

chemical weapon: a chemical, delivered by missile, bomb, or aircraft, that kills, immobilizes, or incapacitates the enemy

cock: the part on a gun that hits the primer or firing pin or explodes the percussion cap to start the firing mechanism; also called a hammer

coffee-mill gun: a mounted hand-cranked machine gun so named because the bullets drop into the weapon from a hopper on top that makes the gun resemble an old-fashioned coffee grinder

crossbow: a bow attached crossways to a stock. Often mechanical means are used to increase the tension on the bow and thus the killing power of the arrow.

cruise missile: a pilotless missile with a jet engine

cylinder: a revolving metal unit on a revolver holding ammunition in separate chambers in readiness for firing

depth charge: an explosive, dropped or fired by a ship, airplane, cannon, rocket, or torpedo, that is set to explode at a certain point under water to attack a submarine

destroyer: a warship that is designed for speed and maneuverability and is armed with mounted guns, depth charges, torpedoes, and missiles; originally intended to destroy submarines

elevator flap: a surface that can be tilted up or down to control vertical movement

flint: a type of quartz that sparks when struck against steel

flintlock: a firing mechanism in a gun in which flint is struck against steel to create sparks that light the priming powder

fulminate of mercury: a chemical compound that explodes when struck

Gatling gun: a multi-barreled machine gun invented by Richard Gatling. The barrels rotate, allowing the gun to fire bullets as fast as a soldier can crank the ammunition-feeding mechanism.

gladius: a short sword used by the Romans in Caesar's time

gunpowder: an explosive powder, usually a combination of potassium nitrate, charcoal, and sulfur

gyroscope: a wheel that rotates on an axis like a spinning top. When suspended in a set of rings, it remains pointed in its original direction regardless of the motion of the rings.

handgun: a firearm that can be aimed and fired with one hand

hatch: an opening on the top of a submarine or ship

hull: the main body of a ship

incendiary bomb: a bomb containing chemicals that burn with extreme heat when the bomb explodes

infantry: soldiers fighting on foot

intercontinental ballistic missile (ICBM): a ballistic missile that is launched into the atmosphere to give it enough range (over 4,000 miles) to target other continents

ironclad: a ship covered in iron armor

javelin: a light spear that is thrown

lance: a weapon with a long wooden shaft and metal point for stabbing

longbow: a bow as long as six feet

machine gun: a gun that fires rapidly and repeatedly. Older models were hand cranked, while modern machine guns fire continuously with the pull of the trigger.

matchlock: a firing mechanism in which a lit piece of twine—a match—ignites the gunpowder, resulting in an explosion that fires the gun

mine: an explosive device, often buried underground or submerged in water, which is detonated by contact, a timed fuse, or remote control

missile: a weapon that is fired or thrown at an enemy target; usually a ballistic missile, which is rocket powered and then free falling, or a cruise missile, which is powered by a jet engine

muzzle: the open end of the barrel on a gun

nuclear weapon: a bomb or warhead whose powerful explosion is caused by nuclear fission (the atomic bomb), which is the division of the nucleus within an atom; or nuclear fusion (the hydrogen bomb), which is the fusion of two or more nuclei

paddle wheel: a wheel composed of fixed paddles that propels a boat through water

patent: a grant made by a government that gives an inventor the sole right to manufacture, distribute, license, or sell an invention for a certain period of time

pepperbox revolver: a handgun that resembles a pepperbox, or pepper shaker. Its six barrels revolve to allow repeated firing without reloading.

percussion system: a firing mechanism for a gun that uses fulminate of mercury or another impact-sensitive explosive to achieve almost instantaneous fire. It received its name because it is activated by striking.

pike: a long spear used by infantry as a thrusting weapon

priming pan: the part of a gun on which the priming powder is placed

priming powder: a fine gunpowder used to ignite the main charge in a firearm

propeller: a device that propels an aircraft or boat with rotating blades that push back air or water when spinning. Virtually all propellers are screw propellers (shaped like a screw), but Bushnell's propeller was modeled on windmill blades.

prototype: a final version of an invention that serves as a model for mass production

radar: short for **ra**dio **d**etecting **a**nd **r**anging, a means of locating an object by measuring the length of time it takes radio waves to strike the object and bounce back

recoil: the "kick" of a gun, caused by the reaction of the gun to the force of firing. A recoil-operated automatic weapon harnesses the energy of the recoil to power the firing mechanism.

revolver: a firearm, usually a handgun, with a revolving cylinder containing a number of cartridges or bullets. Another early type of revolver had several revolving barrels instead of a revolving cylinder.

rifle: a longarm or cannon with a rifled bore, which means the interior of the barrel has spiral grooves that make the bullet spin to achieve accuracy

rigging: a system of supporting cables, ropes, and control lines that support and adjust the mast, other spars, and sails on a ship

rocket: a missile propelled by a rocket engine, which derives force from reaction and can operate in outer space

round: a cartridge, bullet, or other piece of ammunition in a weapon

rudder: a vertical piece of wood or metal that moves side to side to steer a craft right or left

shell: a piece of artillery containing explosives or chemical weapons

shot: a solid projectile designed to be propelled from a firearm or cannon; or, tiny lead or steel pellets that fill a shotgun cartridge

shrapnel: fragments of an exploding shell

spar torpedo: an explosive attached to a long pole

sponson: a container on the side of a tank that houses mounted guns

steam engine: an engine that is powered by the pressure from steam driving the engine's pistons

stock: the handle or support of a firearm to which the barrel and firing mechanism are attached

submarine: a craft that can move completely submerged under water

Subroc: **sub**marine-launched **roc**ket; a rocket-powered torpedo fired from a submarine

tank: an armored vehicle with mounted guns that moves on caterpillar tracks

Tommy gun: a machine gun invented by General John T. Thompson that is powered by blowback, a mechanism involving the gas pressure of the bullets and a spring; also called submachine gun

torpedo: a self-propelled underwater missile that can be launched from a submarine, aircraft, or ship. Fulton's "torpedo" was instead an anchored underwater explosive.

touchhole: an opening at the breech of the barrel in early firearms through which gunpowder is ignited

turret: a revolving structure housing large guns or cannons on top of a warship or tank

warhead: an explosive device mounted on the front end of a missile or torpedo

wheellock: a firing mechanism in a gun in which a piece of iron pyrite is rubbed against a rough-edged wheel to create sparks to light the priming powder

BIBLIOGRAPHY

Abbot, Henry L. *Beginning of Modern Submarine Warfare under Captain Lieutenant David Bushnell.* Hamden, Conn.: Archon Books, 1966.

Addington, Larry H. *The Patterns of War since the Eighteenth Century.* Bloomington, Ind.: Indiana University Press, 1984.

Armstrong, David A. *Bullets and Bureaucrats: The Machine Gun and the United States Army, 1861-1916.* Westport, Conn.: Greenwood Press, 1982.

Batchelor, John, and John Walter. *Handgun: From Matchlock to Laser-sighted Weapon.* New York: Sterling Publishing Company, 1988.

Baxter, James Phinney. *The Introduction of the Ironclad Warship.* Cambridge, Mass.: Harvard University Press, 1933.

Bennett, Frank M. *The* Monitor *and the Navy under Steam.* Boston: Houghton Mifflin, 1900.

Black, Jeremy. *European Warfare 1660-1815.* New Haven, Conn.: Yale University Press, 1994.

Brodie, Bernard. *Sea Power in the Machine Age.* Princeton, N.J.: Princeton University Press, 1943.

Carver, Field Marshal Lord. *The Apostles of Mobility.* New York: Holmes & Meier Publishers, Inc., 1979.

Chapelle, Howard I. "Fulton's 'Steam Battery': Blockship and Catamaran." United States National Museum Bulletin 240. Washington, D.C.: Smithsonian Institution, 1966.

————. *The History of the American Sailing Navy: The Ships and their Development.* New York: W. W. Norton & Company, Inc., 1949.

Chinn, George M. *The Machine Gun: History, Evolution, and Development of Manual, Automatic, and Airborne Repeating Weapons.* Vol. 1. Washington, D.C.: United States Government Printing Office, 1951.

Church, William Conant. *The Life of John Ericsson.* New York: Charles Scribner's Sons, 1911.

De Kay, James Tertius. *The Battle of Stonington: Torpedoes, Submarines, and Rockets in the War of 1812.* Annapolis, Md.: Naval Institute Press, 1990.

Diagram Group, The. *Weapons: An Encyclopedia From 5000 B.C. to 2000 A.D.* New York: St. Martin's Press, 1990.

Dornberger, Walter. *V-2.* New York: The Viking Press, 1958.

Dupuy, Trevor N. *The Evolution of Weapons and Warfare.* New York: Da Capo Press, Inc., 1984.

Edwards, William B. *The Story of Colt's Revolver: The Biography of Col. Samuel Colt.* Harrisburg, Penn.: The Stackpole Company, 1953.

Ericsson, John. "The Building of the *Monitor.*" In *Battles and Leaders of the Civil War.* Vol. I. New York: Thomas Yoseloff, Inc., 1956.

Farley, Karin Clafford. *Robert H. Goddard.* Englewood Cliffs, N.J.: Silver Burdett Press, 1991.

Faulkner, Keith. *Jane's Warship Recognition Guide.* New York: HarperCollins Publishers, 1996.

Flexner, James Thomas. *Steamboats Come True.* New York: The Viking Press, 1944.

Ford, Roger. *The World's Great Handguns: From 1450 to the Present Day.* New York: Barnes & Noble Books, 1997.

Foss, Christopher F. *Jane's Tank and Combat Vehicle Recognition Guide.* New York: HarperCollins Publishers, 1996.

Fuller, J. F. C. *Armament and History.* New York: Charles Scribner's Sons, 1945.

Gray, Edwyn. *The Devil's Device: Robert Whitehead and the History of the Torpedo.* Annapolis, Md.: Naval Institute Press, 1991.

Greene, S. Dana. "In the *Monitor* Turret." In *Battles and Leaders of the Civil War.* Vol. I. New York: Thomas Yoseloff, Inc., 1956.

Griffith, Paddy. *Battle Tactics of the Civil War.* New Haven, Conn.: Yale University Press, 1989.

———. *Battle Tactics of the Western Front.* New Haven, Conn.: Yale University Press, 1994.

Harris, Brayton. *The Navy Times Book of Submarines.* New York: Berkley Books, 1997.

Haven, Charles T., and Frank A. Belden. *A History of the Colt Revolver.* New York: William Morrow and Company, 1940.

Haythornthwaite, Philip J. *Invincible Generals.* Bloomington, Ind.: Indiana University Press, 1992.

Hogg, Ian V. *German Secret Weapons of the Second World War.* New York: Arco Publishing Company, 1970.

———. *Guns and How They Work.* New York: Everest House Publishers, 1979.

———. *The History of the Gun.* New York: St. Martin's Press, 1996.

Hoyt, Edwin P. *Submarines at War: The History of the American Silent Service*. New York: Stein and Day Publishers, 1983.

Hughes, B. P. *Firepower: Weapons' Effectiveness on the Battlefield (1630-1850)*. 2nd ed. New York: Sarpedon, 1997.

———. *Open Fire: Artillery Tactics from Marlborough to Wellington*. New York: Hippocrene, 1983.

Hutcheon, Wallace, Jr. *Robert Fulton: Pioneer of Undersea Warfare*. Annapolis, Md.: Naval Institute Press, 1981.

Keating, Bern. *The Flamboyant Mr. Colt and His Deadly Six-Shooter*. Garden City, N.Y.: Doubleday & Company, Inc., 1978.

Keegan, John. "Hitler's 'revenge weapons.'" In *The Second World War*. New York: Viking Penguin, 1989.

Kemp, Paul. *Underwater Warriors*. Annapolis, Md.: Naval Institute Press, 1996.

Liddell Hart, B. H. *The Tanks*. Vol. 1. London: Cassell & Company, Ltd., 1959.

Low, A. M. *Tanks*. London: Hutchinson & Co., Ltd., 1949.

Manucy, Albert. *Artillery through the Ages*. Washington, D.C.: United States Government Printing Office, 1949.

Massie, Robert K. Dreadnought*: Britain, Germany, and the Coming of the Great War*. New York: Random House, 1991.

Morison, Samuel Eliot. *"Old Bruin": Commodore Matthew C. Perry, 1794-1858*. Boston: Little, Brown and Company, 1967.

Neufeld, Michael J. *The Rocket and the Reich: Peenemünde and the Coming of the Ballistic Missile Era*. Cambridge, Mass.: Harvard University Press, 1995.

Parsons, Wm. Barclay. *Robert Fulton and the Submarine*. New York: Columbia University Press, 1922.

Partington, J. R. *A History of Greek Fire and Gunpowder*. Cambridge, England: W. Heffer & Sons, Ltd., 1960.

Piszkiewicz, Dennis. *The Nazi Rocketeers*. Westport, Conn.: Praeger, 1995.

Pocock, Rowland F. *German Guided Missiles*. London: Ian Allan, Ltd., 1967.

Potter, E. B., ed. *Sea Power: A Naval History*. Annapolis, Md.: Naval Institute Press, 1981.

Roland, Alex. *Underwater Warfare in the Age of Sail.* Bloomington, Ind.: Indiana University Press, 1978.

Rothenberg, Gunther E. *The Art of Warfare in the Age of Napoleon.* Bloomington, Ind.: Indiana University Press, 1978.

Rywell, Martin. *Samuel Colt: A Man and an Epoch.* Harriman, Tenn.: Pioneer Press, 1952.

Spears, John R. *The History of Our Navy.* New York: Charles Scribner's Sons, 1899.

Stine, G. Harry. *ICBM: The Making of the Weapon that Changed the World.* New York: Orion Books, 1991.

Stuhlinger, Ernst, and Frederick I. Ordway III. *Wernher von Braun: Crusader for Space.* Malabar, Fla.: Krieger Publishing Company, 1994.

Swinton, Ernest D. *Eyewitness; Being Personal Reminiscences of Certain Phases of the Great War, Including the Genesis of the Tank.* Garden City, N.Y.: Doubleday, Doran & Company, Inc., 1933.

—————. *Over My Shoulder: The Autobiography of Major-General Sir Ernest D. Swinton.* Oxford, England: George Ronald, 1951.

Von Braun, Wernher, and Frederick I. Ordway III. *History of Rocketry & Space Travel.* 3rd ed. New York: Thomas Y. Crowell Company, 1975.

Wahl, Paul, and Donald R. Toppel. *The Gatling Gun.* New York: Arco Publishing Company, Inc., 1965.

Welles, Gideon. "The First Iron-Clad Monitor." In *Annals of War.* Edison, N.J.: The Blue & Grey Press, 1996.

White, Ruth. *Yankee from Sweden: The Dream and the Reality in the Days of John Ericsson.* New York: Henry Holt and Company, 1960.

Whitehouse, Arch. *Tank: The Story of Their Battles and the Men Who Drove Them from Their First Use in World War I to Korea.* Garden City, N.Y.: Doubleday & Company, Inc., 1960.

Wilson, R. L. *Colt, An American Legend: The Official History of Colt Firearms from 1836 to the Present.* New York: Abbeville Press, 1985.

—————. *The Colt Heritage.* New York: Simon and Schuster, 1979.

Wood, John Taylor. "The First Fight of Iron-Clads." In *Battles and Leaders of the Civil War.* Vol. I. New York: Thomas Yoseloff, Inc., 1956.

Abrams tank (M1A2), 102-103
Ager, Wilson, 78, 79
aircraft carriers, 56, 57
airplanes (military), 56, 57, 87, 123, 124, 125, 126, 127-128
Alexander the Great, 90
Archimedes, 50
Archimedes screw, 50
armor, 9, 10, 90, 91
Armstrong, Neil, 120
Army, U.S., 38, 40, 86, 128
artillery, 8, 12, 13, 106, 107, 108, 126; rocket-powered, 109; shell, 14, 49, 53, 102-103, 113, 117
A7V tank, 101
Asquith, Herbert Henry, 95
Asroc (anti-submarine rocket), 72, 73
atomic bombs, 7
Austrian Empire, 60, 61, 65, 67, 68, 81, 83
Axster, Herbert, 105

Bacon, Roger, 10, 109, 121
balance chamber, 67-68
ballast, 20, 21, 22, 26
ballistic missiles, 7, 12, 15, 29, 72, 105, 107, 112, 113, 117, 118, 119, 120, 121, 128. *See also* ICBMs; rockets
barbed wire, 93, 94, 99, 100
barrel, 10, 11, 12, 91, 108; of machine gun, 76, 79, 83, 84, 87; of revolver, 33, 38
battleships, 14, 54; developed by Ericsson, 45, 46, 49, 50-51, 52-54; replaced by other ships, 56, 57; steam-powered, 48, 49, 50, 52; used in World War I, 55; used in World War II, 55-56. *See also Monitor*
Becker, Karl, 107, 108
Bernoulli, Daniel, 50
Big Willie, 97-98, 99, 100, 101, 102
biological warfare, 8, 127
Blanco Encalada, 70
blowback gun, 84-85, 86, 87
Boer War, 92, 94
Bonaparte, Napoleon, 28
Bourne, William, 19, 21

Bradley fighting vehicles (M2, M3), 103
Braun, Wernher von: death of, 120; early years of, 111; interest of, in space flight, 105, 111, 112; rockets developed by, in Germany, 12, 105, 112-114, 114-118; work of, on U.S. rocket program, 105, 120
broadside sailing ships, 14
Browning, John Moses, 84
B-2 Stealth bomber, 123, 125
Buffalo Bill Cody, 41
bullets, 75, 78-79, 91, 108, 113; metal-piercing, 99; used in machine gun, 82, 83, 87
Bushnell, David: death of, 28; early years of, 18-19; mines built by, 18, 22, 23, 25, 26, 27, 28, 63, 72; propulsion system developed by, 18, 22, 23; submarine developed by, 14, 17, 18, 22, 23; *Turtle* submarine of, used during Revolutionary War, 18, 23-25, 26, 29
Bushnell, Ezra (brother), 18, 19

Caesar, Julius, 8
Cambrai, Battle of, 100-101
Canandaigua, 17
cannons, 13-14, 21, 51, 54, 55, 86, 107, 109; used on tanks, 94, 96, 98, 101
cartridges, 35, 40, 78-79, 84
catapults, 8, 9, 126
caterpillar tracks, 94-96, 97, 101
cavalry, 8, 90-91, 95
chariots, 8, 89, 90, 95
chemical warfare, 127
Churchill, Winston, 94-95, 96, 102
Civil War, U.S., 17-18, 28, 41, 45, 51, 57, 64, 77, 78
coffee-mill gun, 78, 79
Collier, Elisha, 33-34, 35, 38
Colt, Christopher (father), 31-32, 36
Colt, Samuel: death of, 43; early years of, 31-32; factories of, 37, 38, 39, 43; mine designed by, 38, 64; patents acquired by, 12, 36; revolver developed by, 12, 31, 32, 35, 36, 38, 39, 40, 41, 43, 78, 91; as salesman, 31, 35, 36, 37, 38, 40, 43
Comanche Indians, 39, 42

Confederate navy, 17, 18, 46, 51, 52
Congress, 52
Congreve, William, 108, 109, 113, 121
Crimean War, 41, 50
crossbow, 9-10, 91
Cumberland, 52
cylinder (revolver), 33, 35, 38, 40, 42
Cyrus (king of Persia), 89, 90

Day, J., 21, 22
de Luppis, Giovanni, 61-62, 65
de Son (French inventor), 20
destroyers, 14
diving plane, 26
Dixon, G. E., 17
Dormus, Count, 84
Dornberger, Walter: as artillery officer, 107; death of, 120; early years of, 107; rockets developed by, in Germany, 12, 105, 107, 108, 111-114, 115-118; work of, on U.S. rocket program, 105, 120
Dreadnought, 55
Drebbel, Cornelius, 19, 20

Eagle, 24-25
Edison, Thomas, 80, 81
1812, War of, 37, 48, 109-110
elephants, war, 89-90
Ericsson, Brita (mother), 46
Ericsson, John: death of, 57; early years of, 46-47; engines designed by, 47, 49; *Monitor* built by, 14, 45, 46, 51, 52, 54, 91; patents of, 50; in Swedish army, 47; and use of steam power, 48, 49, 51; work of, for U.S. Navy, 50, 51, 52, 54
Ericsson, Olof (father), 46
Exocet missile, 56, 57, 125
Explorer I, 120
Eyewitness, 102

F-15 Eagle, 124
flintlock, 11-12, 22, 32, 34, 38, 91; multi-shot, 32-34
Foch, Ferdinand, 101
F-117A Nighthawk, 124-125

Forsyth, Alexander, 12, 34
France, 28, 50, 51, 61, 68, 81, 92, 115, 128
Fulton, Robert, 14, 26-28, 48, 63, 64, 72
Fulton the First, 48

Gatling, Richard Jordan, 78, 79, 83, 91
Gatling gun, 76, 78-80, 83, 87, 91, 126
George Washington, 29
German, Thomas, 94
Germany, 68, 81, 101, 107, 108, 115; demilitarized after World War I, 12, 106-107; machine guns used by, during World War I, 85, 92-93, 94, 100; rockets developed by, 107, 108, 111, 112-114, 115-118; submarines used by, during World War I, 71-72; V-2 rockets used by, during World War II, 119
gladius, 8
Goddard, Robert, 107
Göring, Hermann, 106
Great Britain, 50, 55, 92, 93, 115, 128; during American Revolution, 23-25; early rockets developed in, 109-110; during Napoleonic Wars, 28, 47; tanks used by, during World War I, 86, 94-98, 99-101; V-2 rocket attacks on, during World War II, 105, 119. *See also* Royal Navy
G7 torpedo, 72
gunpowder, 22, 49, 62; introduced in Europe by Bacon, 10, 109; used in guns, 11, 12, 40, 75, 79; used in rockets, 108-110, 111
guns: early, 10-12, 109; influence of, on warfare, 10, 91. *See also* machine gun; revolver
gyroscope, 70, 113, 117

High-Altitude Area Defense missile, 128
High-Explosive Anti-Tank (HEAT) round, 102-103
Hiroshima, 7, 128
Hitler, Adolf, 105, 106, 115, 119
H. L. Hunley, 17-18
Holland, John P., 71
Hotchkiss gun, 84
Housatonic, 17
Howard, Edward, 34

Huascar, 69
Hunley, H. L., 18

ICBMs, 7, 120, 121; Minuteman III, 120, 121; Peacekeeper, 120; SS-18, 120. *See also* ballistic missiles; missiles
ironclad ships, 14, 45, 46, 49, 50, 51, 52, 59, 61, 63, 65, 69, 70, 73. *See also* battleship; *Monitor*
Ironside, 54
Italy, 60-61, 68

Jackson, Andrew, 37
Japan: battleships of, 14, 55, 56; torpedo boats of, 71
javelins, 8, 89, 90
Jupiter C rocket, 120

Key, Francis Scott, 110
Kitchener, Horatio Herbert, 94, 96

La Gloire, 51, 61
Lee, Ezra, 24-25, 26
Lincoln, Abraham, 78
Little Willie, 97
longbows, 9, 10, 91

McHenry, Fort, 109-110
machine guns, 5, 7, 12, 15, 94; automatic, developed by Maxim, 75, 78, 82-83, 85, 87, 91, 92, 126; blowback, 84-85, 86; early, 78-80, 81; Gatling gun as, 76, 78-80, 83, 87, 91; importance of, 83, 85; M-16, 87; M-2, 87; M-249, 87; powered by gas, 84, 87; recent developments in, 87; speed of, 12, 79, 83, 87; use of, during World War I, 85-86, 91, 92-93, 99, 100; used on tanks, 95, 96, 98, 101
Maine, 2
Mark I tank. *See* Big Willie
Marne, Battle of the, 92
matchlock, 10-11, 12, 91
Maxim, Hiram: airplane built by, 75; automatic machine gun developed by, 12, 75, 76, 78, 81, 82-83, 84, 85, 87, 91, 92;

death of, 86; early years of, 77; as electrical engineer, 75, 80-81; electric lights developed by, 75, 80; patents acquired by, 84
Maxim, Leander (brother), 77
Merrimac, 46, 51. *See also Virginia*
Mexican War, 38, 39, 40, 41
mines, 18, 26, 27, 38, 64; built by Bushnell, 18, 22, 23, 25, 28
missiles, 2, 56, 57, 120, 123, 125-126, 128; ballistic, 7, 12, 15, 29, 72, 105, 107, 113, 118, 119, 120, 128; early development of, 108-110; fired from submarines, 29, 72; ICBMs, 7, 120, 121; recent developments in, 120-121; strategic, 2, 120, 121; tactical, 121; Tomahawk cruise, 56-57, 123, 126, 127. *See also* rockets
Monitor, 14, 45-46, 51, 52-54, 55, 91
M113 armored personnel carrier, 103
M-16 assault rifle, 43
M-2 machine gun, 87
M-249 squad automatic weapon, 87
Musashi, 55, 56
muzzle-loading firearms, 12

Nagasaki, 7
Napoleonic Wars, 28
Nautilus, 26-28
Navy, U.S., 17, 45, 50, 51, 52, 54, 56, 57, 85; submarines used by, 29, 71
Nazis, 105, 115
Newton, Isaac, 75, 108
Nicholas I (Russian tsar), 43
Nimitz, 57, 126
Nordenfeldt, Thorsten, 69, 71
North Atlantic Treaty Organization (NATO), 124, 125
nuclear weapons, 2, 7, 12, 15, 29, 56, 72, 120, 127-128

Odkolek (Austrian army captain), 84
Ohio, 29
Ohio-class submarines, 2, 29
Operation Desert Shield, 87, 103
Operation Desert Storm, 125

paddle wheel, 20, 21, 48, 49, 50
Paixhans, Henri-Joseph, 14, 49
Papin, Denis, 20, 22, 29, 48
Paris gun, 108, 117
Patent Arms Manufacturing Company, 37, 38, 39
patents, 12, 36, 50, 60, 78, 80-81, 84
Peenemünde, 113, 114
pepperbox revolver, 32-33
percussion system, 12, 34, 35, 38, 78, 79
Persian Gulf War, 56, 103, 123, 124, 125, 127
pikes, 91
portholes, 13-14
Pretorius, Johann Christian, 21
Princeton, 50
propellers, 50, 62; used on submarines, 17, 23, 24, 25, 26, 27

radar, 57, 123, 125-126
recoil, 75, 82, 83, 84, 87, 108
Renault tank, 101
Retort, 48
Revolutionary War (American), 14, 18, 23-25, 28, 63
revolvers: Collier, 33-34, 35; developed by Colt, 12, 31, 32, 35, 36, 38, 39, 41, 43, 78, 91; flintlock, 32-34, 38; pepperbox, 32-33; percussion systems used in, 12, 34-35, 38; Single Action Army Model 1873, 31, 32; Walker-Colt, 40, 41
rifled bore, 12, 113
rockets, 72, 107, 108; A series (German), 105, 113, 115, 116-118, 119; developed by Dornberger and von Braun, 12, 105, 111-114, 115-118; early, 108-110; liquid-fuel, 107, 111, 112, 113; in U.S. space program, 120; V-2, 105, 106, 107, 113, 115, 118, 119. *See also* ballistic missiles; missiles
Royal Navy (Great Britain), 28, 47, 49, 55, 68, 69, 94-95
Russia, 41, 50, 68, 71, 81, 85, 120, 128
Russo-Japanese War, 71; machine guns used in, 85, 92

Sahand, 56

Salvator, Franz, 84
Santiago, Battle of, 85
Saturn V rocket, 120
Seawolf-class submarines, 29
Seminole Indians, 38, 39
Shah, 69
Shaw, Joshua, 35
Shepard, Alan, 120
ships: aircraft carriers, 56, 57; destroyers, 14; ironclad, 14, 45, 46, 49, 50, 51, 52, 59, 61, 63, 65, 69, 70, 73; oar-powered, 12-13; sailing, 13-14, 48, 51; steam-powered, 14, 26, 48, 49. *See also* battleships; submarines
Shrapnel, Henry, 109
Single Action Army Model 1873, 31, 32
"smart bombs," 123, 124
"soft bombs," 124
Somme offensive, 99
space flight, 111, 118, 120
Spanish-American War, 85
sponsons, 98, 101
steamboats, 20, 26, 28, 48, 63
steam engines, 46, 47, 48, 49, 50, 59, 60, 61, 65
Strategic Defense Initiative (Star Wars), 128
Strauss, 56
submachine guns, 86. *See also* machine guns
submarines, 2, 7, 14-15, 64, 71; ballast used in, 20, 21, 22, 26; ballistic-missile, 29, 72; depth control of, 20, 21, 26; developed by Bushnell, 14, 17, 18, 22, 23; developed by Fulton, 26-28; early, 19-21, 22; nuclear-powered, 28, 29; Ohio-class, 2, 29; propulsion of, 18, 19, 20, 21, 22, 23, 27; torpedoes fired from, 14, 15, 69, 71-72; used during Civil War, 17-18, 28, 64; used during Revolutionary War, 18, 23-25, 26; used during World War I, 14, 71-72
Subroc missile, 15, 72
Swinton, Ernest, 89; as British officer, 91, 92, 102; caterpillar tracks used by, 94-96; death of, 102; early years of, 92; encouraged by Churchill, 94-95, 96; tank developed by, 12, 85-86, 93, 94-98, 102, 103; as writer, 92, 93, 102

tanks, 7, 15, 91, 126; Abrams, 102-103; Big Willie, 97-98, 99, 100, 101, 102; caterpillar tracks on, 94-96, 97, 101; developed by Swinton, 93, 94-98, 102, 103; Little Willie, 97; machine guns used on, 95, 96, 98; origin of name, 98; recent developments in, 102-103; size of, 97-98, 102; used in World War I, 12, 86, 99-101
Taylor, Zachary, 40
Texas Rangers, 39, 42
Thompson, John T., 86
Tomahawk cruise missile, 56-57, 123, 126, 127
Tommy gun, 86
torpedoes, 7, 14, 63, 123; depth control of, 65, 66, 67-68; developed by Whitehead, 14, 59, 65-66, 67-68, 72, 73; early, 64; fired from subs, 15, 69, 71-72; Fulton's, 27, 28; gyroscope used in, 70, 113; importance of, 68-70, 71, 73; origin of name, 27, 63; recent developments in, 72; spar, 17, 64, 69; used in World War I, 71-72; used in World War II, 56, 68, 72
Trafalgar, Battle of, 28, 47
trench warfare, 12, 86, 91, 93, 99
Trident missile, 29
Tsushima, Battle of, 71
turbo fuel pump, 115, 117
turret, 89, 90; on ships, 14, 51, 53-54, 55; on tanks, 95, 96, 97, 98
Turtle, 18, 23, 24-25, 26, 27, 29

U-boats (*Unterseeboten*), 71-72
Union army, 78
Union navy, 17
United States, 128; missiles used by, 2, 15, 29, 120, 121; and Persian Gulf War, 56, 87, 103; space program of, 120; submarines used by, during Revolutionary War, 12, 24-25, 26; submarines used by, during Civil War, 17-18, 28; tanks used by, 102, 103; war of, with Mexico, 38, 39, 40, 41. *See also* Army, U.S.; Navy, U.S.

Verne, Jules, 26

Versailles, Treaty of, 106
Victoria (queen of Great Britain), 95
Vietnam War, 127
Virginia, 46, 51, 52-54
Vixen, 85
V-1 bomb, 56
von Zwehl, A. D. H., 101
V-2 rocket, 105, 106, 113, 115, 119
Vulcan-Phalanx close-in weapon system, 126

Walker, Samuel Hamilton, 39-40
warheads, 66; nuclear, 2, 7, 12, 15, 29, 56, 72, 120
Warrior, 51, 54
Washington, George, 24, 26
Wells, H. G., 93
wheellock, 11, 12
Whitehead, Frances Maria (wife), 60
Whitehead, James (father), 59
Whitehead, Robert: death of, 71; depth-control devices invented by, 67-68; early years of, 59-60; gyroscope used by, 70, 113; patents acquired by, 60; steam engines designed by, 60, 61; torpedo developed by, 14, 59, 65-66, 67-68, 72, 73; work of, for Austrian navy, 67-68
Wild Bill Hickok, 41
Wilhelm II (German kaiser), 92, 95
Worden, John, 52
World War I, 92, 106, 107, 108; battleships used in, 55; results of, 107; submarines used in, 14, 71-72; tanks used in, 12, 85, 99-101; trench warfare during, 91, 92-93, 99
World War II, 56, 68, 72, 102, 125, 127-128; battleships used in, 14, 55-56; outbreak of, 115; V-2 rocket used in, 105, 119

Yamato, 55, 56
Ypres, Third Battle of, 101
Yugoslavia, 123, 124-125, 127

ABOUT THE AUTHOR

Jason Richie is the author of several titles from The Oliver Press, including *Secretaries of State: Making Foreign Policy* and *Secretaries of War, Navy, and Defense: Ensuring National Security.* A former noncommissioned officer in the U.S. Army, where he gained firsthand experience with some of the weapons in this book, Richie graduated summa cum laude from the University of Minnesota with a degree in American history. He lives in Houston, Texas, with his wife, Diana, and son, James.

PHOTO ACKNOWLEDGMENTS

Archive Photos: pp. 116, 118
Archive Photos/Popperfoto: p. 100
Connecticut State Library: pp. 30, 32, 37 (bottom), 41 (top), 42, 43
Defense Visual Information Center: pp. 29, 87, 120, 121, 122, 124, 126
D. E. Turner, National Museum of Naval Aviation: p. 57
Dictionary of American Portraits (published by Dover Publications, Inc., 1967)**:** p. 78
Edwyn Gray: pp. 58, 62, 66, 68, 69
Harry S. Truman Library: p. 6
Library of Congress: pp. 8, 13, 26, 37 (top), 40, 41 (bottom), 44, 54, 74, 85, 95, 104, 109, 110
London *Times*/Archive Photos: p. 119

National Archives: pp. 86, 92, 106
Revilo: pp. 20, 24, 27, 47, 64, 70
Stay Vertical Designs: pp. 114, 115, 117
The Tank Museum: pp. 88, 97, 98
U.S. Department of Defense: pp. 103, 125, 127
U.S. Department of the Interior, National Park Service, Edison National Historic Site: p. 81
U.S. Naval Historical Center: pp. 52, 53
U.S. Naval Institute: pp. 2, 15, 16, 18, 23, 48, 55, 56, 71, 73
U.S. Postal Service: p. 63
Weapons and Armor (published by Dover Publications, Inc., 1978): pp. 9, 10, 11, 33, 76, 82, 90, 91